THE SYSTEM OF GOVERNMENT
IN ONTARIO

THE
SYSTEM OF GOVERNMENT
IN ONTARIO

GEORGE G. BELL AND ANDREW D. PASCOE
YORK UNIVERSITY

WALL & THOMPSON
TORONTO

Canadian Cataloguing in Publication Data

Bell, George G., 1920-
The system of government in Ontario

Contains pt. 1 and a summary of pt. 2 of: The
Ontario government : structure and functions.
Includes index.
ISBN 0-921332-01-7

1. Ontario - Politics and government. I. Pascoe,
Andrew D., 1962- . II. Bell, George G., 1920-
The Ontario government. III. Title.
JL270.B452 1988   320.4713   C88-093556-1

ISBN   0-921332-01-7
Printed in Canada by John Deyell Company.
1 2 3 4 5   92 91 90 89 88

TABLE OF CONTENTS

PREFACE

Introduction

The purpose of *The System of Government in Ontario* is to provide a succinct overview of the structure of the government of Ontario for the benefit of those who live and work in the province and for those who work in or with the government and need to understand its general framework. The volume is suitable as an introductory synopsis on the Ontario government, or it might be added to the working library of anyone with a need for quick reference to the major divisions of the Ontario government.

The Organization of this Book

The System of Government in Ontario is divided into three sections. The first section describes the Ontario Parliament, including the structure and functions of the Executive and Cabinet Committees; the Legislative Assembly, Legislative Committees, Legislative Offices; and the Judiciary. The second section describes the process of public policy development and budgeting. The third section describes the Ontario Public Service, which encompasses the Central Agencies, Central Ministries, and Line Ministries; and the Agencies, Boards, Commissions, and Special Purpose Bodies. For each central agency and each central and line ministry, a description of its roles and functions is given along with a sketch of its divisional structure, its budget, and the agencies, boards, and commissions which report to it.

Considerably greater detail may be found in *The Ontario Government: Structure and Functions* by George G. Bell and Andrew D. Pascoe (Toronto: Wall & Thompson, 1988) from which this book has been excerpted. In addition to what is found herein, that work gives a more detailed account of the background history; organization; programs; budget; agencies, boards, and commissions; legislation administered; and innovations of each ministry and central agency.

Acknowledgements

It would not have been possible to assemble the necessary information and to coordinate and produce this first edition of *The System of Government in Ontario* without the fullest cooperation of all ministries and central agencies (particularly the staff of the Communications Branches), which is greatly appreciated. Special acknowledgement and thanks go to the Management Policy Division of Management Board Secretariat for their support in the development and publication of this book, and especially to Barry Gardiner, Director of the Policy Development and Administration Branch, for his direction and guidance and for his efforts in coordinating the information assembly and gathering process.

Acknowledgement also goes to the Faculty of Administrative Studies, York University, for their provision of resources for research assistance and computing, and most especially to Gisela Birmingham, whose personal contributions to the assembly, word processing, and administrative management of this project ensured its effective completion. Finally, special thanks to Byron Wall and Keith Thompson, for their creative input, technical expertise and tireless efforts in the final editing and production of this book.

Communications

The currency and accuracy of annual revisions and future editions will depend on an effective two-way process. Therefore, all suggestions and comments as to how to improve *The System of Government in Ontario* will be welcomed by: Professor George G. Bell, Faculty of Administrative Studies, York University, 4700 Keele Street, North York, Ontario M3J 1P3.

G.G.B.
A.D.P.

Section 1
PARLIAMENT IN ONTARIO

Ontario has enjoyed responsible government for over one hundred and fifty years. Today, parliamentary government in the province encompasses three major areas of responsibility: Executive, Legislative, and Judicial.

"Parliament" in Ontario refers to the "formal" executive (the Lieutenant Governor), the "political" executive (the Premier and Cabinet Ministers), the Legislative Assembly and its offices, and the system of judicial courts which exist to settle legal disputes.

In Canada, the distribution of legislative powers between the federal and provincial governments is set out in Sections 91 and 92 of the *British North America Act, 1867,* and the *Constitution Act, 1982.* The limitations and restrictions on the powers of the federal government and the provinces are set out in judicial decisions of the United Kingdom Privy Council prior to 1949 and the Supreme Court of Canada since 1949. (A detailed discussion of the latter may be found in J.R. Mallory, *The Structure of Canadian Government,* 1984, chapters nine and ten.) The Meech Lake agreement between the federal and provincial governments and subsequent constitutional discussions will result in further definition of their respective powers.

This Section of the book describes the structure and functions of the three divisions of Parliament in Ontario: the Executive, which formulates government policy and oversees the public service in the administration of government programs; the Legislature, which enacts, amends, and repeals legislation, authorizes the collection and expenditure of funds, and debates the policies put forth by the Government; and the Judiciary, which adjudicates civil and criminal disputes in the province.

THE LIEUTENANT GOVERNOR AND THE EXECUTIVE

THE LIEUTENANT GOVERNOR

The Queen of Canada is the official Head of State. The Lieutenant Governor is the nominal Head of State at the provincial level, empowered with the responsibility of representing the Sovereign in the province. The real power of governing, however, resides with the Premier and the Executive Council, the elected Members of Provincial Parliament who are appointed as Ministers of the Crown by the Lieutenant Governor on the recommendation of the Premier.

The Lieutenant Governor of Ontario is appointed by the Queen on the recommendation of the Prime Minister of Canada. The document of appointment is signed by the Governor General on behalf of the Queen. The appointment, by tradition, is for a period of five years—or "at the pleasure of the Crown"—and carries the title of "The Honourable" for life. In conversation and correspondence the Lieutenant Governor is addressed as "Your Honour," as is his or her spouse.

The Lieutenant Governor serves in a dual capacity; first as representative of the Sovereign for all purposes of the provincial Government, and second, as a federal officer in discharging certain functions of the Sovereign. The Lieutenant Governor, as Head of State, opens, prorogues (closes), and can dissolve the Legislature. The Lieutenant Governor is responsible for swearing in the Premier and Cabinet Ministers and must ensure that a Government is in office at all times.

The Lieutenant Governor also has the discretionary authority: to select the Premier, for example in the event of the death of the holder of that office; to refuse a request by the Premier for dissolution of the Legislature; or to ignore the advice of the incumbent Premier and Cabinet. The Lieutenant Governor also has the authority to dismiss a Government. Given that much of the Lieutenant Governor's authority is symbolic and ceremonial in nature, such occurrences are rare. The Chief Justice of Ontario acts for the Lieutenant Governor when the latter is unable to do so. One or the other must be in the province at all times.

The Lieutenant Governor must sign (give "Royal Assent" to) all Bills passed by the Legislature before they can become law. The Lieutenant Governor also signs proclamations and appointments of persons to government posts, including provincial judges, crown attorneys, justices of the peace, and commissioners. A major responsibility of the Lieutenant Governor, at the opening of a new session of Legislature, is to deliver the Speech from the Throne, which outlines proposed legislation to be introduced in the forthcoming session.

In addition to formal duties, the Lieutenant Governor engages in a large number of discretionary, but traditional, activities, such as becoming honorary patron to volunteer organizations, sponsoring awards, receiving dignitaries, sending messages of congratulations or condolence, presenting citations, and participating in investitures, dedications, and other major events. The Lieutenant Governor holds receptions, luncheons, and dinners for guests of various occupations, organizations, and professions; receives members of the Royal Family, heads of state, ambassadors, consuls, and other representations of foreign countries; attends religious, cultural, educational, and recreational events; and visits hospitals, senior citizens homes, centres for the disabled, and other public institutions. The Lieutenant Governor is supported in his role by a staff of five in the Office of the Lieutenant Governor.

1987–88 Expenditure Estimate:

Office of the Lieutenant Governor: $416,000.00

THE PREMIER AND OFFICE OF THE PREMIER

The Premier of Ontario is the leader of the governing political party. He or she is the First Minister of Cabinet and President of the Executive Council, the chief Government spokesperson in the Legislative Assembly, and an elected representative of a specific constituency. The Premier makes formal recommendations to the Lieutenant Governor on the appointment of Cabinet ministers, approves the appointment of deputy ministers, and initiates the "Order-in-Council" appointment (Cabinet approval on behalf of the Lieutenant Governor) of approximately one-third of the members of the governing bodies of provincial Crown corporations, agencies, boards, and commissions. The Premier determines the portfolio structure of the Government and the organization of the Cabinet. He or she is the ultimate authority on government policy and the principal advisor to the Lieutenant Governor.

The Office of the Premier is primarily concerned with supporting the Premier as the leader of the Government and as the elected representative of his or her constituents. A functional relationship is maintained between the Premier's Office and Cabinet Office, which supports the Premier as head of the Cabinet. The Premier is supported by two senior staff members of deputy minister rank: a Principal Secretary, who heads up the functions associated with the development and communication of government policy, and an Executive Director, who provides leadership in administrative and appointment matters. Under Premier William Davis, the Premier's Office was headed by a Deputy Minister, Office of the Premier, assisted by an Executive Director. Dr. Edward Stewart, the Deputy Minister, was also "double-hatted" as Secretary of Cabinet. Under Premier David Peterson, the position of Secretary of Cabinet has been separated from the Premier's Office. The staff of the Office of the Premier, numbering approximately forty, are hired on personal service contracts to provide partisan political advice and administrative support.

They are not public servants.

The principal *advisory* functions of the Office of the Premier are: to provide the political policy link between the Premier, all Ministers and ministries, and the major policy committees of Cabinet; to coordinate Government processes consequent to the establishment of policy; to provide input to the Government's legislative program, long-term strategy, and priorities; to coordinate the political processes of the Office; and develop the Lieutenant Governor's Speech from the Throne.

The principal *service* functions of the Office of the Premier are: to budget the Premier's time, schedule and complete travelling arrangements; to maintain relations with the communications media, write speeches and statements; to brief the Premier daily on legislative matters; to receive, record, and reply to correspondence; to handle invitations and appointment requests; to assist with constituency matters; to maintain liaison with caucus members; to deal with inquiries from the public and from special interest groups; and to receive delegations and unscheduled visitors.

1987–88 Expenditure Estimate:

Office of the Premier: $1,977,731.00

CABINET AND CABINET OFFICE

Cabinet is the focal point for decision-making in the Ontario Government, in that it is responsible for initiating, approving, and executing Government policy. Cabinet exists in law as the Executive Council of the Province of Ontario. All ministers are members of Cabinet. The Premier or a designated Minister may serve as chairman of Cabinet. Currently, Cabinet meetings are held every Wednesday.

Cabinet is based on long-standing constitutional convention. As the executive decision-making authority of the Government, Cabinet reflects the notion of responsible government. That is, its members are ultimately accountable to the Legislature and the people of Ontario for the policy, programs, and administration of Government. Cabinet decision-making is by consensus and its documents and deliberations are secret. Ideally, Cabinet membership is structured to reflect the cultural and demographic makeup and regional nature of Ontario society.

Cabinet attempts to set the broad direction and priorities of the Government, decide the content of the Speech from the Throne, and coordinate the Government's legislative program for each session. It also makes decisions on budget and manpower allocations each fiscal year. By its very nature, Cabinet is linked to all ministries and central agencies of Government. Cabinet is supported in its administrative role by several standing and special purpose committees, which bring together matters of policy and administrative concerns at the highest level of decision-making in the Government.

Cabinet size has fluctuated in recent years. For example, one of the major changes to the structure of Cabinet made by Premier Frank Miller in 1985 was to increase its size from 28 under Premier William Davis to 33 members, with the

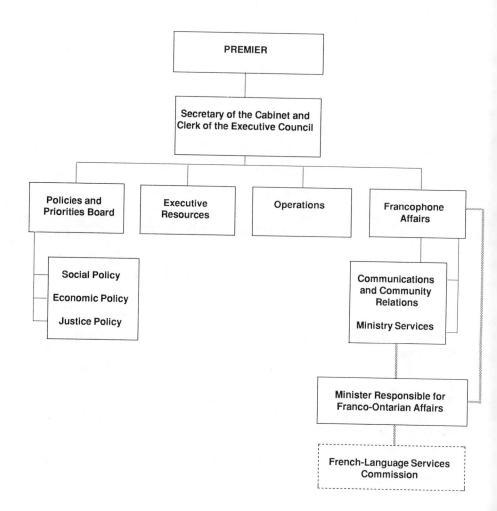

Figure 1
CABINET OFFICE

appointment of seven ministers "without portfolio." This position, much like a federal Minister of State, is designed to fill a special political need, serve as a training ground for future Ministers, or to give extra support to a Minister with major administrative responsibilities and a heavy work load. Conversely, in 1985, Premier David Peterson contracted the size of Cabinet to 21 members by eliminating the Provincial Secretary appointments. These were Cabinet ministers who had overseen the Resource Development, Justice, and Social Development policy fields from 1972 to 1985. Instead he assigned the responsibilities for chairing the Cabinet Committees for Economic Policy, Justice, and Social Policy to three line ministers in addition to their assigned ministerial responsibilities. He also combined several portfolios under selected ministers. After winning a large electoral majority in the 1987 election, Premier Peterson increased the size of Cabinet to 30 members, but continued the practice of "double-hatting" in filling the chair positions for the three Cabinet policy committees.

Cabinet Office is the central agency which provides administrative services and policy analysis for Cabinet and its Committees. Cabinet Office is headed by the Secretary of the Cabinet, who also carries the title of Clerk of the Executive Council. The Office has two main divisions (see *Figure 1*): a Policy Section, under the Secretary of the Policy and Priorities Board, and an Operations Section under the Associate Secretary of Cabinet for Operations. In addition, the Associate Secretary of Cabinet for Executive Resources (who reports to the Premier) and the Executive Director for Francophone Affairs (who reports to the Minister Responsible for Francophone Affairs) are situated within Cabinet Office. Cabinet Office personnel, numbering approximately 100, are all public servants.

The *policy* functions of Cabinet Office are: to undertake expenditure reviews, coordinate the allocation process, and assist the Ministry of Treasury and Economics and Management Board of Cabinet in developing the annual expenditure allocations among the ministries; to review legislative proposals and decisions and draft the Government's legislative program in consultation with the Government House Leader and individual ministers; to assist in the preparation of the Speech from the Throne and the Prorogation Speech; to make briefing arrangements for the Premier, for Cabinet, and Policy and Priorities Board meetings; to analyze submissions, brief Cabinet committee chairmen, prepare the agenda for each committee meeting, and prepare committee reports and recommendations to full Cabinet for policy and ad hoc committees; to coordinate and manage the Government's policy priorities process and large cross-Cabinet issues; and to provide staff support to the Policy and Priorities Board and the Cabinet Committees on Economic Policy, Justice, and Social Policy.

The *operational* functions of Cabinet Office are: to arrange Cabinet and Cabinet committee meetings, to prepare agenda, record discussions and prepare and distribute minutes of meetings, to provide document service for Cabinet, to research and retrieve information for ministries, to monitor implementation of political commitments, to make arrangements for delegations to Cabinet, to organize ceremonial activities such as swearing-in procedures for change of Government or minister(s),

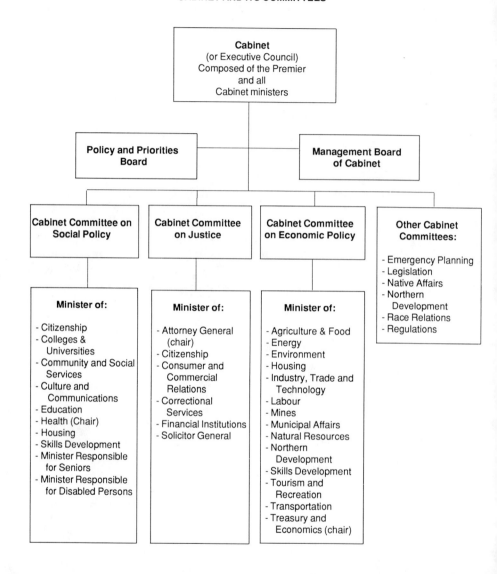

Figure 2
CABINET AND ITS COMMITTEES

Cabinet
(or Executive Council)
Composed of the Premier
and all
Cabinet ministers

Policy and Priorities Board

Management Board of Cabinet

Cabinet Committee on Social Policy

Cabinet Committee on Justice

Cabinet Committee on Economic Policy

Other Cabinet Committees:

- Emergency Planning
- Legislation
- Native Affairs
- Northern Development
- Race Relations
- Regulations

Minister of:

- Citizenship
- Colleges & Universities
- Community and Social Services
- Culture and Communications
- Education
- Health (Chair)
- Housing
- Skills Development
- Minister Responsible for Seniors
- Minister Responsible for Disabled Persons

Minister of:

- Attorney General (chair)
- Citizenship
- Consumer and Commercial Relations
- Correctional Services
- Financial Institutions
- Solicitor General

Minister of:

- Agriculture & Food
- Energy
- Environment
- Housing
- Industry, Trade and Technology
- Labour
- Mines
- Municipal Affairs
- Natural Resources
- Northern Development
- Skills Development
- Tourism and Recreation
- Transportation
- Treasury and Economics (chair)

and to provide liaison with the Lieutenant Governor, the Speaker, the Clerk of the House, the Government House Leader, the Board of Internal Economy, Management Board of Cabinet, and the Ministry of Treasury and Economics.

1987–1988 Expenditure Estimates:

Cabinet Office: $8,657,400.00

Cabinet Committees

The Ontario Cabinet system has evolved from a plenary-style, decision-making body to one where the focus of policy development rests with a number of powerful Cabinet committees. (See *Figure 2*.) This development can be traced to the recommendations of the Committee on Government Productivity (COGP) report of 1972, a watershed review of the structure and operations of the Government of Ontario. COGP foresaw that the growing volume and complexity of policy issues would become unmanageable for any single body of Ministers. A more specialized and accountable system of issues management was considered necessary for the future. It therefore recommended a restructuring of Cabinet and the establishment of several Cabinet Committees. Formally, a Cabinet committee does not make final decisions on policy issues. Instead, it makes recommendations to full Cabinet. Nonetheless, the role of the latter has become, essentially, one of ratification of these recommendations with a minimum of debate, with the occasional need to resolve policy disputes that cannot be settled at the committee level. This evolution reflects the COGP's perceived need to improve the efficiency of the decision-making process within the political executive.

Cabinet submissions normally originate within the staff of a ministry in response to a public concern or a policy initiative of the Government, and are placed before Cabinet by the responsible minister after scrutinization and deliberation by any number of committees (see "The Public Policy Development Process" below). There are two types of Cabinet committees: standing and ad hoc. The former meet regularly and have an ongoing mandate to examine a well-defined set of policy issues. The latter meet periodically to deal with special or unique issues and are disbanded when the problem is resolved.

The standing Cabinet committees include: the Policy and Priorities Board; the Management Board of Cabinet; the Legislation Committee; the Regulations Committee; the Cabinet Committees of Economic Policy, Justice, and Social Policy; as well as other standing committees with more specific mandates.

Policy and Priorities Board

The Policy and Priorities Board is the powerful "inner Cabinet." This committee's purpose is to develop, review, coordinate, and advise on policy and priorities relating to the social and economic needs of the province as reflected by the Government's short- and long-term goals. The "P & P Board" also studies general budgetary and fiscal policy and priorities, including expenditure and transfer payment programs and recommendations submitted by the Cabinet policy committees. The P & P Board oversees the coordination of government-wide issues and projects and attempts to resolve issues that cross governmental, ministerial, or policy committee boundaries. Like other Cabinet committees, with the exception of Management Board of Cabinet, the P & P Board does not make decisions on policy, but recommends courses of action to full Cabinet.

The Board is chaired by the Premier; other members traditionally include the Deputy Premier (if applicable), the Chairman of Management Board of Cabinet, the Treasurer, and four or five other influential ministers. In the Government of Premier William Davis, the Provincial Secretaries of the Resource Development, Justice, and Social Development policy fields, and the Minister of Intergovernmental Affairs also sat on the P & P Board. Premier Frank Miller increased the size of the P & P Board to eleven, but excluded the Provincial Secretaries. The composition of the P & P Board under Premier David Peterson includes eight portfolios (see *Annex F*): the three Chairmen of the Cabinet policy committees—the Deputy Premier (who is also the Minister of Treasury and Economics and the Minister of Financial Institutions), the Minister of Health, and the Attorney General—along with the Chairman of Management Board, the Government House Leader (who is also the Minister of Mines), the Minister of the Environment, the Minister of Housing, and the Minister of Northern Development. The P & P Board usually meets once a week.

The P & P Board, through its membership, links all the central agencies that have responsibilities for policy development and administration. The Board is a final policy review body for most major policy issues prior to full Cabinet consideration. The Board often refers items to Management Board for consideration of financial, manpower, and administrative implications. The P & P Board is served by the Committee of Advisors (consisting of the Deputy Ministers of the member ministries) and a small secretariat of senior civil servants in Cabinet Office. The Committee of Advisors meets before each Board meeting to review and discuss agenda items and to review ministry submissions to be presented at the meeting.

Management Board of Cabinet

Management Board of Cabinet is a key standing committee of Cabinet, concerned with the efficient and effective utilization of public resources. It performs the overall general management function for the Ontario Government on behalf of Cabinet. "Management Board" has four main duties:

1. Managing expenditures by participating in the Government's annual resource allocation exercise;

2. Ensuring probity, prudence, efficiency, and integrity in the conduct of Government business;

3. Establishing overall management, technological, and administrative policies; and

4. Fulfilling the role of "employer" for the Government in collective bargaining with its employees.

Membership on Management Board varies. It usually consists of a Chairman (a Cabinet minister responsible for Management Board), a Vice-Chairman (currently the Deputy Premier, who is also the Minister of Treasury and Economics and the Minister of Financial Institutions), and several other ministers (currently the Ministers of Citizenship, Energy, Environment, and Government Services, the Solicitor General, and the Minister without Portfolio for Senior Citizens'Affairs). The Chairman is traditionally a member of the Policy and Priorities Board. Unlike other Cabinet committees, Management Board can make decisions on resource allocations without approval by full Cabinet, although it may be vetoed. As a rule, Management Board meets once a week, on Tuesday.

The activities of Management Board are supported by two central agencies and a regulatory body: Management Board Secretariat, the Human Resources Secretariat, and the Civil Service Commission (see "Public Service," below).

Legislation Committee

Before receiving final approval from full Cabinet for introduction in the Legislature, Government bills are examined by the Legislation Committee to ensure internal consistency and conformity with Government policy. This Committee also considers the relative priority of bills in terms of the Government's overall legislative program, and reviews private members' bills, motions, and petitions to Cabinet. This Committee currently has seven members: The Attorney General (Chairman); the Government House Leader (who is also the Minister of Mines); the Ministers of Community and Social Services; Industry, Trade and Technology; Municipal Affairs; and Transportation; and the Minister without Portfolio for Disabled Persons. The Committee meets approximately every two weeks.

Regulations Committee

The Regulations Committee reviews all regulations which require the approval of the Lieutenant Governor in Council prior to concurrence by Cabinet and submission to the Lieutenant Governor for signature. The composition of this Committee has varied over time to include only Cabinet ministers, or only parliamentary assistants, or a combination of ministers and parliamentary assistants, or a combination of Cabinet ministers and Members of Provincial Parliament. Currently chaired by the Minister of Labour, it includes the Minister of Consumer and Commercial Relations and seven MPPs. The Committee meets most Mondays.

Cabinet Committees on Economic Policy, Justice, and Social Policy

These committees are responsible for the review and consideration of policy issues and proposals before they are submitted to the Policy and Priorities Board, full

Cabinet or other Cabinet committees. They identify policy issues and coordinate inter-ministerial and intergovernmental activity to ensure appropriate policy and program development within their areas of responsibility. The policy committees meet approximately every other week. They are supported by small secretariats in Cabinet Office which assist with policy development and coordination and liaison within and among the three committees. Although matters before the policy committees can be referred to key central agencies for evaluation, senior representatives from the Ministry of Treasury and Economics, Ministry of Intergovernmental Affairs, and Management Board Secretariat attend the meetings of these committees, in order to monitor policy development and offer assessments of intra-provincial or federal-provincial policy ramifications, budgetary or taxation implications, and administrative issues.

Other Standing Committees

Other standing committees are concerned with specific issues, and are established by the Premier and Cabinet in order to address an emerging policy issue. They oversee policy development in areas that may not be covered in the mandate of a particular ministry, or which transcend either ministerial boundaries or the boundaries of federal and provincial governments. These include the Committee on Emergency Planning, the Committee on Native Affairs, the Committee on Northern Development, and the Committee on Race Relations.

Committee on Emergency Planning: Attempts to coordinate governmental efforts in dealing with emergency situations (e.g. a provincial security problem). It is chaired by the Solicitor General, whose ministry is responsible for emergency planning in the province. The Committee includes 12 ministers. In 1985, Ontario signed a memorandum of understanding with the federal government that ensures federal assistance, when requested by the province, during peacetime emergencies.

Committee on Native Affairs: Coordinates the Government's position for all matters involving native people in Ontario and for all dealings with other governments and organizations in this area. The Committee is chaired by the Attorney General and includes 14 ministers. A Secretariat for Native Affairs is attached to the Ministry of the Attorney General.

Committee on Northern Development: Coordinates the Government's position on all matters involving Northern Ontario, and reviews the impact of Government policies and programs that affect Northern Ontario. The Committee is chaired by the Minister of Northern Development and includes 13 ministers.

Committee on Race Relations: Coordinates the Government's policies on all matters involving race relations, and receives reports from the race relations program commissioner in the Ontario Human Rights Commission. The Committee is chaired by the Minister of Citizenship and includes 11 ministers.

Ad Hoc Committees

Ad hoc Cabinet committees are created to deal with special issues, and are dissolved when the solution to a problem is reached. There are no ad hoc Cabinet committees at present, but recent examples include the committees on Municipal Assessment Taxation and Grants, on Manpower, and the Ontario Bicentennial Commission.

Figure 3
THE ONTARIO LEGISLATURE

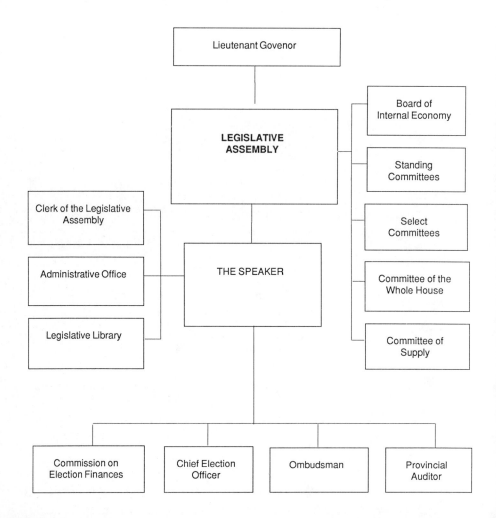

THE LEGISLATURE: ASSEMBLY, COMMITTEES AND OFFICES

Legislative Assembly

In a parliamentary system, the general role of the legislative branch is to refine and legitimize major government policies and proposals for expenditure and taxation, to audit and critique government actions and hold the government accountable, to constitute a representation of the province's political, economic, and social interests, and to form a focal point for debate of society's major issues. In contrast with the federal bicameral system (House of Commons and Senate), Ontario and the other provinces have unicameral parliaments. The Legislative Assembly in Ontario (see *Figure 3*) consists of 130 Members of Provincial Parliament ("MPPs"), elected from 130 electoral districts, for a period of no longer than five years. The Speaker of the Assembly, an MPP from the Government party, who is appointed by the Legislature, is the presiding officer, and is responsible for the policy and operations of the Legislature.

Structure

The "Government" is formed by the political party able to elect or obtain the support of a majority of the representatives to the Assembly. By custom and tradition, the leader of the majority party normally becomes Premier.

In certain circumstances where the party winning the election does not have a clear majority, the opposition parties may combine to form a coalition government or develop through collusion an "accord" whereby one of the opposition parties agrees under a set of negotiated conditions to support a minority government formed by the other opposition party, rather than allowing the party which gained the most seats in the election to govern. This rare phenomenon occurred in 1985, allowing the Liberal party under David Peterson to form the Government.

The Premier selects Cabinet ministers, the most influential group of MPPs, from his or her "caucus" (those party members elected to the Legislative Assembly). The Lieutenant Governor formally appoints Ministers to the Cabinet. The next tier in the Government hierarchy comprises the members who act as "Parliamentary Assistants" to cabinet ministers. As these members fill in when their Cabinet ministers are absent from the House, they must be able to answer for the policies and programs of their ministry. The remaining members of the Government caucus are the "Backbenchers." These members have less direct influence. Nonetheless, through chairmanships of and participation in Legislative committees, these individuals can have a significant impact on Government legislation and resolutions. They also can make input to Government deliberations through discussion in caucus.

The Opposition side is made up of the "Official Opposition" (the party with the second highest number of seats), and the third party in the Ontario political system. At the top of the hierarchy within each of these two groups is the party leader; then a "Shadow Cabinet," consisting of critics of various Government portfolios; then the backbenchers. Opposition MPPs are primarily responsible for ensuring accountability of the Government, exercised through participation in House debate, written questions, Question Period, and Legislative committees.

House leaders and party whips come from each of the three caucuses—Government, Opposition, and third party. They are responsible for coordinating and executing the strategy and tactics of their party with respect to passage of bills, legislative agenda, and debate in the Legislature. When the House is in session, the three House leaders and three party whips meet weekly to determine the agenda for the next week. This coordinating activity is led by the Government House Leader and is based on the legislative program reflected in a report from the meetings of the Legislative Committee of Cabinet.

Sessions

Each annual session of the Legislature is opened by the Lieutenant Governor, who reads the Speech from the Throne, which is a document prepared by Cabinet Office within the parameters identified by the Premier and Cabinet. The Throne Speech states the Government's political philosophy, policy proposals, and legislative program for the new session. There are times when sessions of the Legislature, generally scheduled for March to June and October to December, run longer than scheduled. This is particularly true at Budget time or during debates on major policy issues, when discussion may spill over into periods when the House is normally in recess. Each session of the Legislature is closed by the Lieutenant Governor's Prorogation Speech.

Legislative Process

There are several steps involved in passing a bill into law. At "first reading" there is no debate or vote: the Minister introducing the bill makes an explanatory statement, and background information is distributed. At "second reading" the general principles of the bill are debated in the House. A vote may be taken at second reading to pass or kill a piece of legislation, or it may be passed on to the "Committee of the Whole House" (see below) or to a standing committee for refinement. In the former, minor amendments to the bill may be made during a clause-by-clause examination, without direct public input. In contrast, Legislative committees allow for appearances by public interest groups and concerned citizens. On average, forty percent of Government bills are sent to a Legislative committee for refining after second reading. Finally, after either a second reading vote or examination by the Committee of the Whole House and/or a standing committee, the bill gets "third reading," and may then be passed on to the Lieutenant Governor for signing. Such "Royal Assent" commonly takes place immediately after third reading, but in some cases proclamation may be delayed. Upon "Royal Assent", the bill becomes law. (See *Figure 5*, the Policy Implementation Approval Process flow chart.)

The Legislature deals with three types of legislation. The most important are Government or public bills, which encompass major Government policy proposals, spending or tax measures, and routine governing items, and are introduced by a Cabinet minister. Secondly, the Legislature may examine certain "private members' public bills." These are usually proposals to amend public statutes, put forth by a private member, not a minister. As they have not received Cabinet sanction, such bills cannot involve the spending or taxing of money. They are rarely introduced and even more infrequently passed; many never make it to first reading. Of those that do, most get left on the order paper when a session dissolves, because they do not carry enough priority to become Government policy. The best private members' bills usually become Government bills, and are therefore more likely to pass into law. The final type of legislation is the private bill, which can be introduced by any MPP. These bills concern the activities and interests of a particular group, corporation, profession, or municipality. They are generally considered to be non-controversial, and almost always pass into law.

Legislative Committees

Legislative Committees are an important feature of the legislative process, and are essential to the conduct of business in the Legislature. In Ontario, there are several types of Legislative Committees which review legislation, scrutinize budget estimates, and undertake special studies or investigations: The Board of Internal Economy, Standing Committees of the Legislature, and Select Committees. Two other Legislative "Committees" refer to the whole Legislative Assembly when it is engaged in certain committee-like functions. These are the Committee of the Whole House and the Committee of Supply.

The Board of Internal Economy: A permanent committee, the Board was created under the *Legislative Assembly Act*. The Board is responsible for the approval and management of the budgets of the Legislative Assembly and its Committees and Offices, as well as approval for the organization and staff establishment of the Offices of the Legislature. The Board is composed of seven members: a Chairman (The Speaker of the House), three Cabinet ministers, and one member each from the Government, the Opposition, and the third party. The Board meets approximately every three weeks when the House is in session.

Standing Committees of the Legislature: These are bodies crucial to the performance of the Legislature's policy development and accountability roles. These Committees, composed of Members drawn from each political party and chaired by a Government MPP (except Public Accounts), are created and given areas of jurisdiction at the beginning of each Session. Standing committees meet according to a set schedule, from one to three times a week, as long as the Legislature is in session, and report to the House on matters referred to them. Standing committees are automatically terminated at the end of each Session. At present there are four major standing committees in the Legislature: Administration of Justice, Resources Development, Social Development, and General Government. Other minor standing committees include Public Accounts, Legislative Assembly, Government Agencies, Finance and Economic Affairs, Regulations and Private Bills, and Ombudsman.

Select Committees: These are non-permanent, ad hoc bodies set up to examine or investigate particular issues. Once the task is complete, select committees report to the House, and are dissolved. Recent examples include the Select Committee on Retail Store Hours and the Select Committee on Constitutional Reform.

Committee of the Whole House: This is the term used to refer to the Legislative Assembly when it sits in the Legislative Chamber to debate certain issues, such as a clause-by-clause examination of a piece of legislation after second reading, or bills arising out of the Budget. All MPPs are members of the "Committee of the Whole." The Deputy Speaker takes the chair when the Committee of the Whole House is in session, and, generally, the rules of procedure are more relaxed.

Committee of Supply: This is the term used to refer to the Committee of the Whole House when it is considering the "Estimates"—the annual expenditure budgets of the ministries and central agencies of the government.

Membership in standing and select committees is, ideally, proportional to party standings in the Legislature. Ministers are never members of Legislative committees. Meetings of Legislative committees are generally informal; they are open to the public and the press, and presence of MPPs from all parties is an implicit requirement for any meeting. This can create problems when the composition of the House is in imbalance, as minority parties may find it difficult to contribute adequately to all committee meetings. Under these circumstances, parties with a limited number of MPPs usually find it necessary to assign a member to more than one committee, and to provide for alternates.

Offices of the Legislative Assembly

There are a number of offices and positions unique to the legislative branch of the government that are crucial to its operation. The offices of the Legislative Assembly (see *Figure 3*) include: Speaker of the Legislative Assembly, Clerk of the Legislative Assembly, Legislative Assembly Administration Office, Office of the Chief Election Officer, Commission on Election Finances, Legislative Library, Office of the Ombudsman, and Office of the Provincial Auditor.

Speaker of the Legislative Assembly

A member of the Government caucus, the Speaker is elected by the Assembly in its first meeting after a general election to preside over its meetings, adjudicate, and enforce parliamentary procedures and rules ("standing orders"). The Speaker, in essence a Minister responsible for the policy and operations of the Legislature, is responsible under the *Legislative Assembly Act, 1974* for the Office of the Clerk of the Legislative Assembly, the Legislative Assembly Administration Office, and the other major offices of the Legislature listed below. The Speaker has traditionally been nominated and acclaimed by the Legislative Assembly through an understanding between the Premier and the Leader of the Opposition.

Clerk of the Legislative Assembly

A public servant of deputy minister status, the Clerk advises the Speaker and members of the Legislature on questions of procedure and interpretation of rules and practices of the House. The Clerk is supported by the Office of the Clerk of the Legislative Assembly, which coordinates daily publication of the Orders and Notices, Votes and Proceedings, and Daily Business papers. These documents contain matters before the House, and are the official records of the activities of the Legislature. The Office of the Clerk provides record-keeping services for the Legislature and for Legislative committees, ensures the safekeeping of such papers and records, and handles public enquiries concerning the status of legislation, parliamentary procedure, and issues pertaining to standing and select committees.

Legislative Assembly Administration Office

The Administration Office provides personnel and associated administrative services for each MPP and his or her staff, the three party caucus offices, MPP constituency offices, and other offices of the Legislative Assembly. Branches of the Administration Office include:

Finance Branch provides administrative support, purchasing, supply management, printing, accounting, payroll, and the coordination of constituency offices.

Human Resources Branch provides personnel services for the Legislative Assembly, Legislative offices, and MPPs. The 276 staff of the Legislature are employees of the Legislative Assembly. They are not public servants, nor are they unionized.

Information Services Branch coordinates the Members Office Automation/Networking System, the Parliamentary Public Relations Office (which provides public tours, information, and interpretation services), and the Ontario Legislative Television Service.

Hansard Reporting Service covers the sittings of the Legislative Assembly and committees, and publishes an official report, *Hansard*, which is distributed to all MPPs and most libraries.

Office of the Chief Election Officer

This Office conducts provincial elections under the *Ontario Election Act*. The Office coordinates the appointment, training, and payment of Returning Officers and other election officials, reports election returns, and arranges the rental, equipment, and supply of the polling stations in the 130 electoral districts during an election. The Office maintains an index of provincial election districts by street name and number, and publishes historical information on elections, Legislatures, Cabinets, and political candidates.

Commission on Election Finances

This Commission administers the *Election Finances Act, 1986*, which provides for registration of political parties, riding associations, and candidates for elections, by-elections, and leadership conventions. The Commission supervises limits on campaign expenses, political contributions to registered parties, constituency associations, and candidates, and imposes a time limit on political advertising during an election campaign. The Commission provides subsidies for campaign expenses to eligible candidates and political parties, and collects audited financial statements of parties, riding associations, and candidates.

Legislative Library

The Library provides reference and information services to Members of Provincial Parliament and their staff, officers of the Legislative Assembly, research officers of the three parties, and members of the Legislative Press Gallery. It also provides research services exclusively for MPPs. The Library has an extensive collection of Ontario, Canadian, other provincial, and American government publications, as well as major daily and weekly newspapers and a press clipping service.

Office of the Ombudsman

The Ombudsman administers the *Ombudsman Act*. An officer of the Legislature of Ontario, the Ombudsman is appointed by the Lieutenant Governor in Council on the advice of the Assembly for a period of 10 years. His or her function is to investigate any decision, recommendation, act, or omission made in the administration of any ministry, agency, board, commission, or tribunal of the Government of Ontario. The Ombudsman reports annually to the Speaker. Concerns can be raised, in writing, by any Ontario resident, through any one of eight regional offices. The staff is multilingual. The *Ombudsman Act* does not apply to municipalities, hospitals, school boards, the judiciary, or to the Executive Council.

Office of the Provincial Auditor

Appointed under the *Audit Act*, the Provincial Auditor's major responsibility is to audit the financial statements of the Province, all government ministries, and a number of provincial agencies, boards, and commissions. The Auditor's primary goal can be described as helping the Legislature hold the Government accountable for the management of the province's resources. This goal is achieved through the presentation of the Auditor's Report to the Legislature each year. This report is reviewed by the Legislature's Public Accounts Committee, which summons ministers and senior officials to discuss issues raised by the report. The Auditor's secondary goal is to help deputy ministers and heads of Crown agencies by reporting on the quality of the management of funds in their organizations. The Office of the Provincial Auditor is divided into several branches: Economic Policy, Justice, Social Policy, General Government, Reporting and Standards, Electronic Data Processing and Resources, and Administration. The Office employs approximately 110 staff, the majority of which are professional accountants.

1987–88 Expenditure Estimates:

Legislative Assembly		$ 68,081,000
which includes:.		
Office of the Speaker:	$ 689,100	
Clerk of the Assembly:	4,535,000	
Commission on Election Finances:	1,220,000	
Legislative Library:	4,440,000	
Chief Election Officer:		$ 551,600
Office of the Ombudsman:		6,546,700
Provincial Auditor:		6,699,800

For further information on legislative support services and the remuneration of MPPs, see Annex A and Annex B.

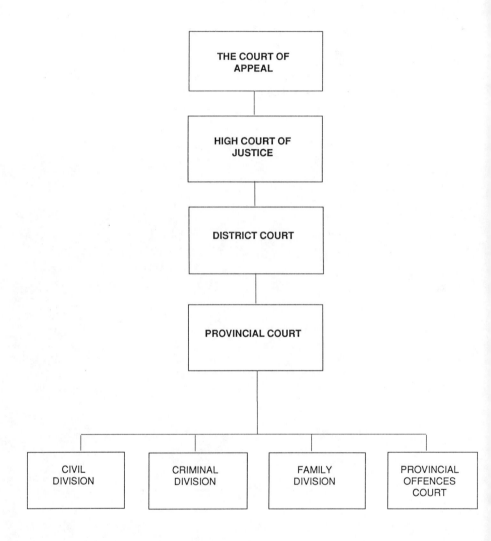

Figure 4
THE JUDICIARY IN ONTARIO

THE COURT OF
APPEAL

HIGH COURT OF
JUSTICE

DISTRICT COURT

PROVINCIAL COURT

CIVIL
DIVISION

CRIMINAL
DIVISION

FAMILY
DIVISION

PROVINCIAL
OFFENCES
COURT

THE JUDICIARY

The Judiciary is the system of courts which the state provides to settle legal disputes arising between individuals, between individuals and the state, and between different levels of government. The primary role of the Judiciary is to provide a forum for the impartial interpretation and application of legal rules and principles, derived from statutes, custom, and precedent. Under the Canadian Constitution, the administration of justice is designated as a provincial responsibility which encompasses the constitution, maintenance, and organization of both civil and criminal courts at the provincial level, with jurisdiction over matters arising under provincial and federal laws.

The appointment of judges, however, is a divided responsibility. The Governor General of Canada, on the advice of the Privy Council, appoints judges for the Superior and District Courts in the province, while the Lieutenant Governor, on the advice of the Attorney General and Cabinet, appoints the judges for the Small Claims, Surrogate, and Provincial Courts. The organization of the Ontario court system is governed by the *Courts of Justice Act*, which establishes the province's courts and regulates their proceedings. As the senior law officer in the province, the Attorney General is responsible for the administration of the court system in Ontario. Advice to the Attorney General can be provided by the Ontario Courts Advisory Council, the Judicial Council of Ontario, and the Inspector of Legal Offices. In general, all court hearings are open to the public. The judicial system in Ontario for both civil and criminal matters is structured hierarchically (see *Figure 4*).

The Supreme Court of Ontario

The Supreme Court of Ontario is the superior court, in the sense that it is not subject to supervisory control by any other court except by due process of appeal. The Supreme Court is divided into two sections:

1. *The Court of Appeal:* The highest court of final resort in the province, it generally hears civil and criminal appeals from the lower courts, or questions referred to it by the provincial government. It is comprised of the Chief Justice of Ontario, his Associate Chief Justice, and 14 other Justices of Appeal. Proceedings take place primarily in Toronto and are generally heard by three judges, who decide cases by majority.

2. *The High Court of Justice:* This is the trial division of the Supreme Court, comprised of the Chief Justice of the High Court, his Associate Chief Justice, and 60 judges. With certain exceptions, such as family matters, parties

before the High Court of Justice may be granted trial by judge and jury. The Divisional Court is a division of the High Court with jurisdiction to hear appeals from provincial administrative tribunals and from Provincial Small Claims Court. The Family Law Division of the High Court handles divorce trials and motions for child custody and support. There is a local office of the Supreme Court in every county and district in the province.

The District Court of Ontario

The District Court has civil and criminal jurisdiction, and is subject to review by the Superior Court. The District Court consists of the Chief Justice of the District Court, the Associate Chief Justice, and 163 judges, including a senior judge for most counties, districts, and judicial districts in the province. In civil cases, any amount of damages may be claimed, but the action may be moved from the District Court to the Supreme Court for an amount over $25,000. District Court hears appeals of decisions of the Provincial Court (Family Division), Provincial Court (Criminal Division), Provincial Offences Court, and Youth Court. It can also try persons charged with an indictable offence. Sheriffs serve documents, summon jurors, and administer the court houses in the 12 Judicial Districts, 11 Districts and 26 Judicial Counties in the province. District Court judges also serve as judges of the Surrogate Court in their district or county. The Surrogate Court considers matters relating to the validity of wills and the administration of the estates of persons who die intestate.

The Provincial Court of Ontario

The Provincial Court is divided into four sections:

1. *Provincial Court (Civil Division):* also known as Small Claims Court, adjudicates damage actions, disputes over goods and services, or claims for outstanding debts, where the amount claimed or the value of property does not exceed $3,000 in Metropolitan Toronto, or $1,000 elsewhere in the province. Procedures in Small Claims Court are generally informal; representation by a lawyer is not required. Referees of the Small Claims Court are available to counsel individuals on their claims.

2. *Provincial Court (Criminal Division):* deals with persons charged with offences under the Criminal Code of Canada, in a trial setting. This court also sits preliminary hearings to determine sufficiency of evidence, bail hearings, and appeals from Provincial Offences Court. Under the federal *Young Offenders Act,* this Provincial Court may sit as Youth Court to try young offenders, 16 or 17 years of age, charged with criminal offences. There are approximately 160 judges in the Criminal Division.

3. *Provincial Court (Family Division):* has jurisdiction over family law matters such as spousal and child support, child custody and access, criminal restraining orders, guardianship, child protection, and adoption. When a young offender (aged 12 to 15) is involved, this division may also sit as

Youth Court, though matters may be referred to the Criminal Division. There are approximately 60 judges in the Family Division.

4. *Provincial Offences Court:* tries persons charged with offences under the Statutes of Ontario, particularly the *Highway Traffic Act.* Proceedings are usually heard by a Justice of the Peace, who is a judicial officer supervised by a provincial judge.

Beyond the provincial court system, a resident of Ontario may have recourse to the federal court system in certain matters, for example, appeals to the Supreme Court of Canada.

Section 2
POLICY DEVELOPMENT AND BUDGETING

The processes by which Government policies are developed and approved, and the collection and allocation of the resources necessary for the implementation of Government programs, are the subjects of this Section.

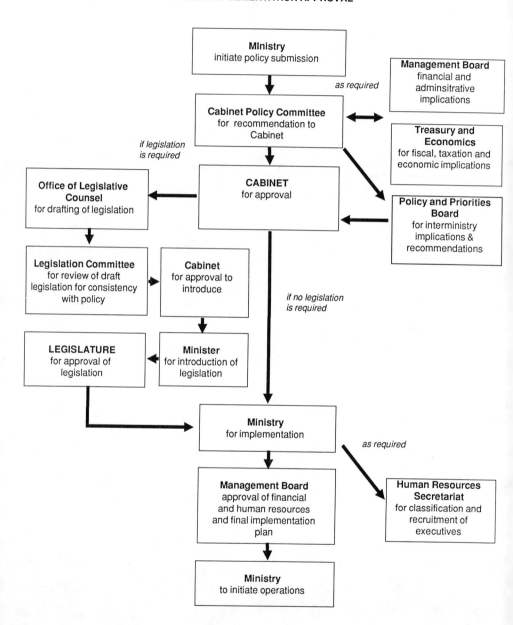

Figure 5
POLICY IMPLEMENTATION APPROVAL

THE PUBLIC POLICY DEVELOPMENT PROCESS IN THE GOVERNMENT OF ONTARIO

A policy is a definite course of action developed to meet identified needs and to address existing and emerging issues. Policies are developed at many levels in the public sector, and may be divided into three general categories:

1. *Public policy* has a direct impact on the public through provincial government program delivery.

2. *Strategic or tactical policy* is designed to deal with a specific situation.

3. *Management policy* comprises operational and administrative directives designed to improve effectiveness of management of the government.

Although public policy-making is ultimately a Cabinet responsibility carried out by elected representatives, the policy development process involves both ministers and senior public servants. The staff support Cabinet decision-making by supplying the best available information, advising ministers, implementing policies, and administering programs.

Sources of Public Policy Ideas

The most common source of public policy ideas in Ontario is the public service, which among its other duties, is responsible for offering policy advice to the Government. Each ministry has a management committee comprised of the Deputy Minister, Assistant Deputy Ministers, and key branch Directors. The management committee meets on a regular basis and recommends the development of policy papers in response to a perceived inadequacy of a particular government program or policy. The research, analysis, and development of public policy issues is usually delegated to the Policy Branch within each ministry. Often government program and policy development is initiated within the public service as a result of contact between senior public servants and outside public interest groups.

Cabinet Ministers and Cabinet Committees often initiate policy development and debate at the Executive level. One of the primary functions of the Cabinet Committees of Economic Policy, Social Policy, and Justice, is to anticipate emerging public policy issues and to initiate the study of these issues by Cabinet Office and by individual ministries. This is particularly important when a public policy issues crosses the jurisdiction of more than one ministry. Inter-ministry committees are often created to study a problem or policy issue that involves several ministries, reporting back to the appropriate Cabinet policy committee. For example, development of provincial policy on industrial waste disposal might involve the Ministries of the Environment, Municipal Affairs, Natural Resources, and Industry, Trade and Technology.

Public policy initiatives can also originate with the policy advisors to the Premier and to Cabinet ministers in response to the influence of interest groups. Often, these issues are a reflection of the governing political party's policy platform. Within the Government caucus, a private member's bill or a caucus committee report may prompt the Government to develop a policy proposal. Royal Commissions or Task Forces often recommend public policy which the Government incorporates into its program. The Opposition may suggest a policy that the Government considers popular or pragmatic. The Press may advocate public policies through the expression of opinions, editorials, and letters to the editor. Finally, a Government may act upon the urging and suggestions of public interest groups.

Analysis and Discussion of Public Policy Proposals

Once the public policy initiative has been researched, analyzed, examined, debated, and developed into a proposal, the management committee of the ministry responsible for the issue will approve or reject the submission of the policy to the appropriate Cabinet policy committee for analysis and discussion. As demonstrated by *Figure 5*, the policy submission may be referred by the Cabinet policy committee to Management Board Secretariat, for an assessment of financial and/or administrative implications, or to the Ministry of Treasury and Economics for an assessment of fiscal and taxation implications. Once approved by the policy committee, the proposal is forwarded to the Policy and Priorities Board for discussion. As the most powerful Cabinet committee and the centre of public policy debate in the Cabinet, the P & P Board decides whether or not to proceed with a policy issue, and makes its recommendation to full Cabinet.

Policy Implementation

Once approved by Cabinet, a policy will be implemented by the appropriate ministry on the basis of an Order-in-Council, a Cabinet directive signed by the Premier and the Chairman of Cabinet. If enabling legislation is required, it will be drafted and submitted to the Cabinet Legislation Committee for review, to ensure consistency with already existing Government policy and programs. The Legislation Committee makes its recommendations to full Cabinet, which must approve the legislation for introduction into the Legislative Assembly by the Cabinet Minister responsible for the policy. The Legislature will then debate the legislation (see *Legislative Process,* above), which must pass it by majority before it can be proclaimed law and passed on to the responsible ministry for implementation.

Before a public policy issue can become a government program, the responsible ministry may have to submit it to the Human Resources Secretariat for approval of staffing, and must submit it to Management Board for final approval of financial and human resources. Only then can the ministry initiate operations. This process may take as long as several months, even years, depending on the perceived urgency and political ramifications of the policy issue. Debate may delay passage at the Cabinet committee level, in the central agencies and ministries, or in the Legislative Assembly.

The policy development and approval process is most effective when it assists in resolving identified issues, satisfies established policy objectives, and meets public needs; when it supports and responds to the political decision-making system in a democratic, responsible system of government; when it respects approved administrative procedures designed to assign specific responsibilities to ministries and central agencies; and when it ensures participation of all appropriate individuals within and beyond government.

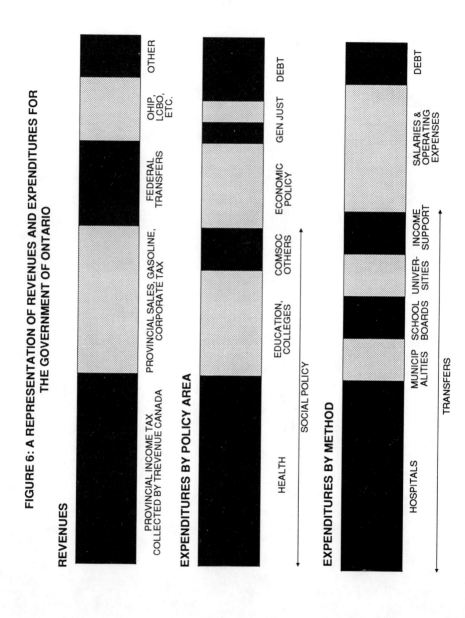

FIGURE 6: A REPRESENTATION OF REVENUES AND EXPENDITURES FOR THE GOVERNMENT OF ONTARIO

REVENUES

PROVINCIAL INCOME TAX COLLECTED BY TREVENUE CANADA | PROVINCIAL SALES, GASOLINE, CORPORATE TAX | FEDERAL TRANSFERS | OHIP, LCBO, ETC. | OTHER

EXPENDITURES BY POLICY AREA

HEALTH | EDUCATION, COLLEGES | COMSOC OTHERS | ECONOMIC POLICY | GEN JUST | DEBT

SOCIAL POLICY

EXPENDITURES BY METHOD

HOSPITALS | MUNICIP ALITIES | SCHOOL BOARDS | UNIVER- SITIES | INCOME SUPPORT | SALARIES & OPERATING EXPENSES | DEBT

TRANSFERS

BUDGETING IN THE ONTARIO GOVERNMENT

The Budget Process

The annual revenue and expenditure (or "estimates") budgeting process in Ontario can take up to 18 months from initial planning in the Ministry of Treasury and Economics to final approval by the Legislative Assembly. The Policy and Priorities Board of Cabinet examines documents placed before it by Treasury and Economics, which outline provincial fiscal strategies based on current economic data, and sends its recommendations to full Cabinet for discussion. Following Cabinet approval, Treasury and Economics, Management Board Secretariat, and Cabinet Office produce a summary document, which sets out specific targets for government expenditure, revenue, and cash requirements, taking into consideration decisions on spending and transfer payments by the federal government. This process is usually completed by August each year so that the estimates process can begin by September.

The estimates process involves the approval of the allocation of funds among ministries, by Cabinet, and of the allocation of money for specific programs by each ministry, in consultation with Management Board Secretariat and Treasury and Economics. By January, detailed estimates are submitted to Management Board of Cabinet. The Estimates are tabled in the Legislative Assembly in May and are debated by the Committee of the Whole House (as the Committee of Supply) and other relevant Legislative committees, ministry by ministry, throughout the year.

The revenue Budget, by contrast, is centred on the Provincial Treasurer and the Ministry of Treasury and Economics, in consultation with the Premier and with private sector financial advisors and special interest groups. The Treasurer generally "brings down" a Budget—a speech in the Legislative Assembly on provincial economic policy and tax changes—in April or May each year, after four to six months of research and preparation. The Budget statement is generally a reflection of Government policies presented in the Speech from the Throne at the beginning of the Legislative session, and outlines the Government's fiscal and economic priorities.

Sources of Revenue

Taxation raises approximately 66 percent of the $34.2 billion of revenue the government will collect in the 1987–88 fiscal year. Half of the taxation revenue, approximately $11 billion, is raised through personal income tax, collected on behalf of the province by the federal Department of National Revenue. The rest of the province's tax revenue is collected by the Ministry of Revenue through the retail sales tax, corporation tax, gasoline and diesel tax, and other taxes. Federal government transfer payments of approximately $5 billion account for a further 15 percent of provincial revenue in Ontario, while miscellaneous revenue such as OHIP premiums, provincial fees, licenses and permits, LCBO profits, and interest on investments account for a further 14 percent of revenue. The final 5 percent of provincial revenue comes from trust revenues and repayment of provincial loans.

Expenditures

Social policy ministries account for approximately 65 percent of provincial government spending, with Health accounting for half this amount, approximately $11 billion of the government's $35.2 billion expenditure budget in 1987–88. Education and Colleges and Universities account for a further one-third of social policy spending, while Community and Social Services and the other Social policy ministries round out the 65 percent share. Spending on Economic policy ministries accounts for 17 percent of the provincial expenditure budget, while General Government ministries and Justice ministries account for 4 percent and 3 percent of expenditures respectively. The final 11 percent of the expenditure budget, close to $4 billion annually, goes to "service," or pay interest on, the provincial public debt of $37 billion. For 1987–88, the provincial budget deficit, or "net cash requirement" stands at approximately $1 billion.

Transfers account for 70 percent of provincial expenditures, with 27 percent going to hospital and medical services, 11 percent to municipalities, 11 percent to school boards, 9 percent to universities and community colleges. Income support such as Welfare and Family Benefits, and other transfers account for the final 12 percent of government transfer expenditures. The salaries and operating expenses of the public service account for 19 percent of expenditures. The final 11 percent of expenditures goes to the public debt.

For a detailed breakdown of the 1987–88 Expenditure Estimates, refer to the individual ministries listed in Part Two of this book.

Section 3
THE PUBLIC SERVICE
IN ONTARIO

The policies developed and monitored by the Executive, Legislative, and Judicial divisions of Parliament in Ontario are *implemented* by the much larger Ontario Public Service. This Section describes the institutions of government and those created by government which implement government policy. The public service includes the central agencies and the central and line ministries of the government. Other government policies are implemented by agencies, boards, commissions, inquiries, and other special purpose bodies created by government.

THE STRUCTURE OF
THE PUBLIC SERVICE

The general role of the public service in the province of Ontario is to provide policy advice to the Premier, Cabinet, and individual ministries, and to administer policies approved by the Legislature. The provincial public service includes approximately 68,000 "classified" staff who are employed on a full-time basis, and a further 15,000 unclassified staff, who are appointed for a defined term (contract) on a part-time or full-time basis.

The labour rights of non-managerial public servants are guaranteed by the *Crown Employees Collective Bargaining Act* and the collective agreements negotiated between the Human Resources Secretariat and such large unions as the Ontario Public Service Employees Union. Ontario public servants are not permitted to engage in certain political activities; they must also take an oath of allegiance to the Crown and an oath of secrecy. Government employees are not permitted to strike. They rely, instead, on a two-stage process of mediation and binding arbitration. The public service in Ontario is structured into central agencies, central ministries, and line ministries.

CENTRAL AGENCIES

For the purposes of this book, the central agencies of the government are those offices which coordinate and manage government activity, each working within its own sphere of responsibility with a common purpose of supporting Cabinet and the line ministries. Although they account for only one percent of the population of the public service, Cabinet Office and Management Board of Cabinet play a role in coordinating and managing Government decision-making disproportionate to their size.

Cabinet Office

Perhaps the most important of all central agencies, Cabinet Office provides staff support to Cabinet and Cabinet committees. For a more detailed description of Cabinet Office, see "Cabinet," above. The duties of Cabinet Office include: arranging Cabinet meetings, preparing the agendas, recording discussion and preparing minutes, analyzing ministry submissions, briefing committee chairman, preparing

Throne Speech and Prorogation Speech, and coordinating the annual expenditure budget. The planning and research capabilities of the once-independent Provincial Secretariats, which were dissolved in 1985, have been incorporated into Cabinet Office by the Government of Premier David Peterson.

Management Board of Cabinet

"Management Board" performs the overall general management function for the Ontario Government on behalf of Cabinet (see "Cabinet Committees," above). Its activities are supported by:

1. *Management Board Secretariat:* The Secretariat supports Management Board by developing guidelines for government-wide management and administrative practices, administering the annual estimates (budgeting) process, coordinating program implementation, monitoring expenditures and program results, and providing advice to Cabinet and its committees on a range of financial, program, and administrative matters. Management Board is structured into three divisions: Management Policy, Programs and Estimates, and Information Technology.

2. *Human Resources Secretariat:* The Secretariat is the corporate advocate for promoting and ensuring that systems are maintained to support the best practices in human resources management by: developing policies, programs, and initiatives in consultation with ministries, providing advice to Management Board, and acting on behalf of the Government in collective bargaining and employee relations matters. The Human Resources Secretariat is organized into three divisions: Employee Relations and Compensation, Corporate Services, and Planning and Development.

3. *Civil Service Commission:* The Commission monitors the performance of the Government as an employer, with particular emphasis on protecting the merit principle and developing corporate values on matters such as conflict of interest and employee ethics. The Civil Service Commission consists of a full-time chairman and four commissioners.

1987–88 Expenditure Estimates:

Cabinet Office: $ 8,657,000.00
Management Board: 208,654,338.00
  including Management Board Secretariat,
  Human Resources Secretariat, and the Civil
  Service Commission.

CENTRAL MINISTRIES

Central ministries are those which perform functions and provide advice on policy development, coordination, and implementation on an overall government basis. These include the Ministries of Treasury and Economics; Intergovernmental Affairs; Revenue; Government Services; and the Attorney General.

Ministry of Treasury and Economics

The Ministry of Treasury and Economics evolved from the Ministry of Treasury, Economics and Intergovernmental Affairs (TEIGA), which operated from 1972–1978. Treasury and Economics advises the government on general fiscal, economic, and regional policies, and provides advice to ensure consistency among these policies and other government programs. The Ministry plays a strategic role in the development of the provincial Budget, coordinates regional economic development policy, and controls provincial borrowing and management of cash resources, statistical information, and the provincial public debt. The Treasurer influences government policy as a member of the Cabinet's Policy and Priorities Board and Management Board, and as Chairman of the Cabinet Committee on Economic Policy.

Divisions:
Office of the Treasury
Office of Economic Policy
Office of the Budget and Intergovernmental Finance Policy
Administration

Number of agencies, boards, and commissions: 4, including:
Stadium Corporation of Ontario
Teachers' Superannuation Commission

Approximate number of public servants: 390
Approximate expenditure budget: $4.4 billion

Ministry of Intergovernmental Affairs

Created in 1978 as a central ministry, the Ministry of Intergovernmental Affairs (MIGA) concentrates on identifying and advancing Ontario's interests and on conducting relations between the Government of Ontario and the federal government, other provincial governments, governments abroad, and their representatives in Ontario. MIGA provides advice and assistance on various areas of intergovernmental policy to all Ontario government ministries. Given the nature of intergovernmental affairs, the Premier typically plays a more active role in MIGA than in other ministries. In fact, since 1985, the Minister of Intergovernmental Affairs has been the Premier.

Divisions:
International Relations
Federal/Provincial Relations
Planning and Management
Office of Protocol.

Number of agencies, boards, and commissions: 5, including
Ontario-Quebec Permanent Commission

Approximate number of public servants: 70
Approximate expenditure budget: $7 million

Ministry of Revenue

The chief function of the Ministry of Revenue is to collect the revenue necessary for the continued operation of government, by administering the major taxing statutes of Ontario. The Ministry conducts property value assessments to provide a tax base for Ontario municipalities, administers several income redistribution programs and the small business development program, and operates the Province of Ontario Savings Office.

Divisions:
Tax Revenue
Property Assessment
Information Technology
Corporate Resources

Approximate number of public servants: 3900
Approximate expenditure budget: $736 million

Ministry of Government Services

The Ministry of Government Services (MGS) is concerned with virtually every aspect of the working environment in the government, and provides central support services to the government as a whole. Its functions include the provision of services to government ministries (payroll and employee benefits, computing services, human resource planning, purchasing, government mail, and information technology), administration of government real estate holdings (acquisition, construction, renovation, maintenance, leasing, and disposal), coordinating government contracts, and delivering customer services to the public.

Divisions:
Supply and Services
Realty Group
Computer and Telecommunications Services
Finance and Administration

Number of agencies, boards, and commissions: 1
Public Service Superannuation Commission

Approximate number of public servants: 2900
Approximate expenditure budget: $521 million

Ministry of the Attorney General

The Ministry of the Attorney General is responsible for the administration of justice in Ontario, and ensures the effective operation of the courts system across the province. The Ministry conducts and regulates all civil litigation and criminal prosecutions for and against the Government. Staff lawyers, on secondment to the Legal Branches of the line ministries, advise heads of ministries and agencies in their legal matters. The Attorney General is the law officer of the Executive Council, and advises the Government and attends to all matters of a legislative nature.

Divisions:
Civil Law
Criminal Law
Courts Administration
Programs and Administration
Policy Development

Number of agencies, boards, and commissions: 6, including
Ontario Law Reform Commission
Ontario Municipal Board
Criminal Injuries Compensation Board

Approximate number of public servants: 3400

Approximate expenditure budget: $347 million

For a fuller discussion of the background, roles and functions, organization, programs, budget, agencies, boards, commissions, and legislation covered by each central agency and central ministry see George G. Bell and Andrew D. Pascoe, *The Ontario Government: Structure and Functions* (Toronto: Wall & Thompson, 1988), from which this book has been excerpted.

LINE MINISTRIES

Line ministries deliver services to the residents of the province. The Committee on Government Productivity (COGP) Report of 1972 recommended reorganization of many line ministries. It also introduced the title of Ministry (to replace that of Department), in recognition of a Minister's responsibility not only for a line department but also for the agencies, boards, and commissions associated with that department. The chief administrative officer of a ministry is the deputy minister, who is appointed by the Premier. While the number and organization of the ministries has been modified since 1972, the basic structure of government continues to be based on the principles and structural concepts established at that time. Typically, line ministries are structured hierarchically into divisions (under assistant deputy ministers, executive directors, or executive coordinators, depending on the size and the role of the division), branches (under directors), and sections (under managers or section heads). (See Figure 7.)

The legal basis of a ministry is defined by an "organic" statute, which establishes the ministry (e.g. *Ministry of Revenue Act*), and a set of "programmatic" statutes (e.g. *Topsoil Preservation Act*), which delineate the general scope of the Ministry's policy responsibilities. A list of line ministries, by policy area, with a brief description of their general function, follows.

Each of the ministries and offices which report to a minister has its own structure and mandate. In the following chapters, the ministries are grouped by the three policy areas: economic policy, justice, and social policy. A brief description is given of the roles and functions of each ministry within its respective category.

ECONOMIC POLICY MINISTRIES

Ministry of Agriculture and Food

The Ministry of Agriculture and Food is responsible for encouraging an efficient and competitive agriculture and food sector and for enhancing the natural and human resources of this sector for the well-being of all the people of Ontario. The Ministry administers farm assistance, foodland preservation, crop insurance, marketing, technology development, and educational and research programs. The Ministry also operates a Consumer Information Centre, which responds to agriculture, horticulture, and food information requests from consumers.

Divisions:
Finance and Administration
Marketing and Standards
Technology and Field Services

Number of agencies, boards, and commissions: 26, including
Agricultural Council of Ontario
Ontario Food Terminal Board
Agricultural Research Institute of Ontario

Approximate number of public servants: 1700
Approximate expenditure budget: $559 million

Ministry of Energy

The Ministry of Energy ensures that Ontario has an adequate and secure supply of energy that meets the needs of Ontario residents and industry, at reasonable prices, in a manner consistent with the protection of the environment. To fulfill this responsibility the Ministry works with other ministries and agencies of the government and with the private energy sector. Major functions include reviewing and advising on energy matters and policy; maintaining liaison between the government and Ontario Hydro; applying policy by coordinating the government's energy-related activities that support research, development, and demonstration of energy technologies; promoting effective and efficient use of energy; and, intervening on energy matters before federal and provincial tribunals.

Divisions:
Energy Policy and Planning
Programs and Technology
Communications and Management Services.

Figure 7
A TYPICAL MINISTRY

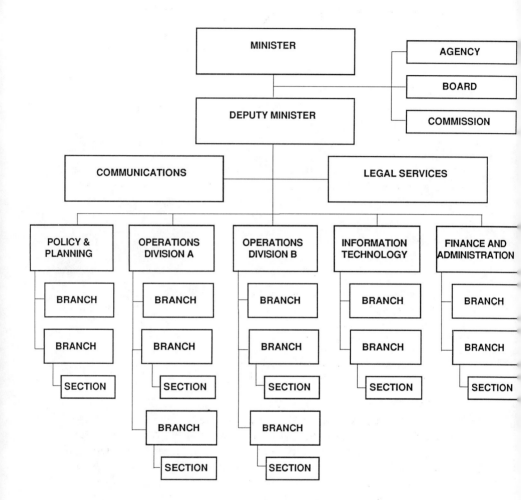

Number of agencies, boards, and commissions: 3, consisting of
Ontario Hydro
Ontario Energy Board
Ontario Energy Corporation

Approximate number of public servants: 220

Approximate expenditure budget: $44 million

Ministry of the Environment

The goal of the Ministry of the Environment is to achieve a quality of the environment (including air, water, and land) that will protect human health and the ecosystem and will contribute to the well-being of the people of Ontario. The Ministry of the Environment is primarily concerned with the regulation, implementation, and enforcement of the environmental standards and guidelines set out in such Acts as the *Ontario Water Resources Act* and the *Environmental Assessment Act.* Although the Ministry develops policy standards and guidelines, and provides laboratory services, the majority of its work is in the field, where Ministry staff enforce policy and ensure that industry, institutions, local governments, and other potential polluters are meeting environmental requirements.

Divisions:
Environmental Services
Intergovernmental Relations and Strategic Projects
Operations
Corporate Resources

Number of agencies, boards, and commissions: 10, including
Environmental Assessment Board
Ontario Waste Management Corporation

Approximate number of public servants: 1700
Approximate expenditure budget: $412 million

Ministry of Housing

The Ministry of Housing is responsible for strategies to help meet the need for affordable rental housing. While encouraging the conservation of existing accommodation, it provides rent-geared-to-income housing for qualified low- and moderate-income households through the Ontario Housing Corporation and helps support municipal, private, and cooperative non-profit housing. The Ministry also administers rent review legislation; helps ensure that all structures in Ontario are built safely and efficiently by developing and maintaining the Ontario Building and

Plumbing Code; and, is responsible for strategies to strengthen Ontario's building industry.

Divisions:
Building Programs
Corporate Resources
Housing Policy
Social Housing

Number of agencies, boards, and commissions: 4, including
Residential Tenancy Commission
Building Industry Strategy Board
Ontario Housing Corporation

Approximate number of public servants: 900

Approximate expenditure budget: $366 million

Ministry of Industry, Trade and Technology

The Ministry of Industry, Trade and Technology (MITT) encourages accelerated introduction and application of new manufacturing technology; assists in product innovation and commercialization of new products and processes; promotes investment, both domestic and foreign; encourages companies to export; supports trade through international offices, trade shows, and missions; promotes and assists the formation of small businesses; and, encourages expansion of the domestic market by identifying domestic sources of supply. In all its activities, the Ministry supports the growth of productive and stable employment in consultation and partnership with the private sector.

Divisions:
Industry and Trade Expansion
Policy and Technology
Small Business Services and Capital Projects
Northern Ontario Industry
Administration

Number of agencies, boards, and commissions: 12, including
Ontario Research Foundation
Ontario International Corporation
3 Ontario Development Corporations
7 Technology Centres

Approximate number of public servants: 640
Approximate expenditure budget: $254 million

Ministry of Labour

The responsibility of the Ministry of Labour is to help ensure equity and social justice for working men and women in Ontario. Its programs and services, through which the Ministry fulfills its mission, are concerned with the rights and responsibilities of the individual worker and the rights and obligations of management and labour in ensuring health and safety in the workplace.

Divisions:
Finance and Administration
Industrial Relations
Labour Policy and Programs
Occupational Health and Safety.

Number of agencies, boards, and commissions: 20, including
Worker's Compensation Board
Ontario Labour Relations Board
Pay Equity Commission

Approximate number of public servants: 1500
Approximate expenditure budget: $104 million

Ministry of Municipal Affairs

The Ministry of Municipal Affairs ensures municipalities have the legislative authority to respond to changing conditions and local needs. Management and administrative support is made available as required along with financial assistance to 839 municipalities across Ontario, which vary greatly in size, structure, and circumstances. The Ministry also encourages sound planning at the community level and renewal activity in municipalities through operational and technical assistance. The Ministry's objectives are achieved through the regulatory and monitoring process as well as by grant and loan programs. Staff assistance and advice is also provided to municipalities and business improvement organizations.

Divisions:
Community Planning
Municipal Affairs
Ontario Municipal Audit Bureau

Number of agencies, boards, and commissions: 1
Niagara Escarpment Commission

Approximate number of public servants: 420
Approximate expenditure budget: $929 million

Ministry of Natural Resources

The goal of the Ministry of Natural Resources is to provide economic and social benefits to the people of Ontario through an effective mixture of both development and conservation of the province's natural resources. These resources include land, water, forests, and wildlife. Encouraging the development of natural resources is a particularly vital objective, since resource-based industries are essential to the health of provincial, regional, and local economies. A great many communities depend largely on such resource industries as fisheries, forestry, trapping, or tourism. The Ministry of Natural Resources seeks to promote the use of available supplies of fish, furbearing animals, aggregate and fuel minerals, and trees, by the resource products industries. In addition, the Ministry seeks to stimulate the development of Crown land, as well as water resources, and to stimulate the production of fish and wildlife in order to promote tourism. The Ministry identifies and supports new market opportunities for resource products and developments. The Ministry of Natural Resources also provides Ontario with protection from forest fires, floods, and erosion.

Divisions:
Forest Resources
Lands and Waters
Outdoor Recreation
Field Operations
Administration

Number of agencies, boards, and commissions: 12, including

Provincial Parks Council
Ontario Forestry Council

Approximate number of public servants: 3700
Approximate expenditure budget: $531 million

Ministry of Northern Development and Mines

The Ministry of Northern Development and Mines is partially or wholly responsible for the delivery of Ontario Government programs in the North relating to: road, rail, air, and water transportation, medical, dental services, fire protection, water, sewage, and drainage systems. The Ministry maintains administrative and program implementation staff in the North, as well as a network of 30 Northern Officers providing "one window" government service to residents of communities across the North. The Ministry is also responsible for encouraging and regulating the orderly development and utilization of the Province's mineral resources.

Divisions:
Northern Development
Mines and Minerals
Planning and Administration

Number of agencies, boards, and commissions: 1
Ontario Northland Transportation Commission

Approximate number of public servants: 440
Approximate expenditure budget: $243 million

Ministry of Tourism and Recreation

The mandate of the Ministry of Tourism and Recreation is to strengthen, maintain, and assist the recreation and tourism industries in the province of Ontario. The Ministry of Tourism and Recreation has two main purposes; first, to enhance and encourage the tourism industry in Ontario; second, to ensure adequate opportunities for recreation, sport, and fitness are available to all residents of the province.

Divisions:
Community Programs/Sports and Recreation
Tourism
Tourism and Recreation Operations
Planning and Administration

Number of agencies, boards, and commissions: 12, including
Metropolitan Toronto Convention Centre
Ontario Lottery Corporation
Ontario Place Corporation
Niagara Parks Commission

Approximate number of public servants: 650
Approximate expenditure budget: $185 million

Ministry of Transportation

The Ministry of Transportation is responsible for the operation and maintenance of the province's highway system, and for most forms of transportation which receive financial support from the province. It manages the municipal transfer payment programs, which provide subsidies for the construction, rehabilitation, and maintenance of municipal roads, as well as the capital and operating costs of municipal transit systems. Through its regional and district staff, the Ministry also provides guidance and expertise to the municipalities in identifying their road and transit needs. Among its other areas of responsibility are fuel conservation and alternative fuels research, inter-city transportation, and goods distribution systems. In addition, it operates three "modal" offices, which promote Ontario's interest in the federally-regulated jurisdictions of air, marine, and rail transportation.

Divisions:
Finance and Administration
Engineering and Construction
Highway Operations and Maintenance

Provincial/Municipal Transportation
Safety and Regulation
plus five regional operations divisions.

Number of agencies, boards, and commissions: 3, including
GO Transit
Ontario Highway Transport Board

Approximate number of public servants: 8500

Approximate expenditure budget: $1.8 billion

JUSTICE MINISTRIES

Ministry of the Attorney General

The Ministry of the Attorney General is a central ministry with some line ministry duties. It is discussed under the heading Central Ministries above.

Ministry of Consumer and Commercial Relations

The Ministry of Consumer and Commercial Relations is responsible for regulating interactions between consumers and businesses in Ontario. The Ministry is responsible for over fifty Acts and related regulations which affect many businesses and virtually every citizen in the Province. The Ministry's objectives include licensing, registration, and inspection of business establishments to promote a high level of ethical business conduct; licensing and inspection of technical and operational situations to ensure public safety; registration of documents related to all aspects of real and personal property ownership; collecting data and providing an efficient system of public information in the registration of vital statistics, property, and companies; applying standards for public entertainment in the areas of film, lotteries, athletics, and horse-racing; and developing and operating an efficient and socially responsible system of liquor distribution and licensing, by controlling the use and availability of beverage alcohol.

Divisions:
Business Practices
Registration
Technical Standards
Support Services

Number of agencies, boards, and commissions: 5, including
Liquor License Board
Ontario Racing Commission
Ontario Film Review Board

Approximate number of public servants: 1700
Approximate expenditure budget: $127 million

Ministry of Correctional Services

The role of the Ministry of Correctional Services is two-fold: to provide opportunities for offenders under sentence to adjust their behaviour in keeping with society's expectations, and to provide society with protection from unlawful behaviour. The Ministry is responsible for male and female persons over the age of 18 who are sentenced to prison terms of less than two years or probation terms of up to three years. It is also responsible for persons on remand awaiting trial or sentencing, persons being held for immigration hearings or deportation, and those awaiting transfer to federal institutions. Under the federal *Young Offenders Act,* the Ministry holds the responsibility for sixteen- and seventeen-year-old offenders, up to their eighteenth birthday. Those offenders under sixteen years of age are the responsibility of the Ministry of Community and Social Services.

Divisions:
Corporate Services
Operations

Number of agencies, boards, and commissions: 1
Ontario Parole Board

Approximate number of public servants: 5900
Approximate expenditure budget: $364 million

Ministry of Financial Institutions

The purpose of the Ministry of Financial Institutions is to consolidate and strengthen the functions pertaining to the regulations, supervision, and policy direction of financial institutions operating in Ontario. The Ministry covers regulation and policy areas relating to loan and trust companies, insurance companies, credit unions and cooperatives, and mortgage brokers, and works closely with the Ontario Securities Commission and the Ontario Pension Commission, which report to the Ministry.

Divisions:
Finance and Administration
Deposit Institutions
Insurance

Approximate number of public servants: 300
Approximate expenditure budget: $37 million

Ministry of the Solicitor General

In fulfilling its responsibilities for law enforcement and public safety in Ontario, the Ministry of the Solicitor General provides the following services: supervision of police services and training throughout the province; a provincial police force with expertise in criminal and traffic law enforcement; specialized scientific criminal analysis; the maintenance of an adequate standard of fire safety services in the province; the determination of causes of death in unusual circumstances; forensic pathology services; and the provision of anatomical materials to schools of anatomy in Ontario. The Ministry is also responsible for ensuring that municipal police forces and the Ontario Provincial Police are effective in preventing and detecting crime and that they enforce the law in a fair and impartial manner.

Divisions:
Program Resources
Policy Development
Public Safety
Ontario Provincial Police (OPP).

Number of agencies, boards, and commissions: 6, including
Fire Code Commission
Ontario Police Commission

Approximate number of public servants: 6200
including approximately 4500 in the OPP.

Approximate expenditure budget: $394 million

SOCIAL POLICY MINISTRIES

Ministry of Citizenship

The Ministry of Citizenship is responsible for encouraging individuals to participate in the Province's economic, political, social, and cultural life and for promoting racial harmony and understanding. Ministry activities aim to ensure that cultural groups, immigrants, newcomers, Francophones, and Native people are able to participate fully in Ontario society, through programs that promote equality of opportunity and access to services, the retention and sharing of cultural traditions, and community development. The Ministry is also responsible for the *Ontario Human Rights Code*.

Divisions:
Citizenship

Number of agencies, boards, and commissions: 2, consisting of
Ontario Human Rights Commission
Advisory Council on Multiculturalism and Citizenship

Approximate number of public servants: 260
Approximate expenditure budget: $40 million

Ministry of Colleges and Universities

The role of the Ministry of Colleges and Universities is to help universities and colleges achieve their goals through programs of operating and capital support. The Ministry administers support funds to 15 provincially assisted universities, Ryerson Polytechnical Institute, the Ontario College of Art, the Ontario Institute for Studies in Education, and 22 colleges of applied arts and technology (CAATs), which operate from 96 campuses throughout the province. MCU also administers student financial assistance programs. To promote accessibility to post-secondary education, funding is provided to all qualified students to remove financial barriers and assist them in obtaining a post-secondary education. The Ministry provides both need-based and merit-based funds to meet the educational needs of those who have completed their secondary school programs.

Divisions:
College Affairs and Student Support
University Relations and Research Support

Number of agencies, boards, and commissions: 4, including
Ontario Council for University Affairs
College Relations Commission

Approximate number of public servants: 240
Approximate expenditure budget: $2.4 billion

Ministry of Community and Social Services

The Ministry of Community and Social Services is one of the largest ministries in the Ontario government. It serves over half a million adults, children, and families across the province who have special requirements. The Ministry offers a broad range of services, from ensuring that the basic needs for food, clothing, and shelter are met, to providing income support, counselling, rehabilitation services, and residential care. The Ministry's primary philosophy is to maintain the stability and quality of life of Ontario society, by strengthening the capacity of communities to cope with change and to respond to the needs of families and individuals in ways that reinforce their dignity and independence.

Divisions:
Community Services
Family Services and Income Maintenance
Operations
Information Systems and Applied Technology
Finance and Administration

Number of agencies, boards, and commissions: 8, including
Child Welfare Review Committee
Social Assistance Review Board

Approximate number of public servants: 8900
Approximate expenditure budget: $3.5 billion

Ministry of Culture and Communications

The Ministry of Culture and Communications promotes shared values, cultural expression, and a multi-cultural heritage by supporting cultural and multi-cultural development in Ontario. The Ministry attempts to support and strengthen all sectors of the cultural community through programs that promote cultural expression and diversity, heritage preservation, library and information services, and formal and informal learning opportunities. The Ministry also represents Ontario's interests in the communications field through its involvement in the federal policy-making process.

Divisions:
Culture
Communications
Finance and Administration

Number of agencies, boards, and commissions: 13, including
Art Gallery of Ontario
Royal Ontario Museum
Ontario Science Centre

Approximate number of public servants: 400
Approximate expenditure budget: $222 million

Ministry of Education

The Ministry of Education oversees the provision of elementary and secondary school education through more than 750 school boards throughout Ontario. It also operates correspondence courses and schools for the deaf, blind, and handicapped. The Ministry is responsible for determining general education policy in the elementary and secondary schools of the province.

Other Ministry responsibilities include providing broad guidelines for the curriculum of Ontario schools; approving the list of textbooks from which school boards make selections for schools; establishing requirements for student diplomas and certificates; setting requirements for and issuing teaching certificates; distributing the funds allocated by the Legislature for assisting school boards with the costs of operating schools; and making regulations to govern the school year and holidays of students, the organization of schools, and the duties of teachers and school board officials.

Divisions:
Learning Services
Learning Programs
Corporate Planning and Policy
Administration

Number of agencies, boards, and commissions: 5, including
Education Relations Commission
Council for Franco-Ontarian Education
Provincial Schools Authority

Approximate number of public servants: 1500
Approximate expenditure budget: $4.4 billion

Ministry of Health

The Ministry of Health is responsible for legislation, policy, funding, programs, services, and facilities deemed essential and appropriate for the prevention of disease, the promotion of health, the protection of community health, and the care, treatment, and rehabilitation of the sick and disabled in the province.

More specifically, the Ministry ensures that communities are covered by, or have access to, basic health services and programs, and that there are the boards, commissions, and agencies needed to oversee their successful operation, provincially and locally; it determines the appropriate allocation of government funds needed for the provision of essential health programs, services, and facilities in accordance with established needs and priorities for prevention and treatment; and it establishes and maintains the provision of insured hospital, medical care, and related services for all residents of Ontario.

The Ministry of Health provides research, analysis, and planning for determining the most effective utilization of resources necessary for the operation of the province's health care system; establishes standards, guidelines, and minimum requirements for community health services and programs, and the provisions for monitoring and maintaining such standards; monitors and assesses health and disease trends and population factors in the province with reporting and statistical systems so as to anticipate and respond in an effective way to changes, trends, or health emergencies as they arise; and ensures that the public is provided with information on Ministry policies, programs, and services as well as information on health hazards and health practices for protecting and promoting health.

The Ministry funds and administers such programs as health insurance, care for the mentally ill, extended health care, home care services, drug programs, and the regulation of hospitals and nursing homes. It operates psychiatric hospitals and medical laboratories and provides funding and professional support for local public health services.

Divisions:
Community Health
Emergency and Special Health Services
Institutional Health
Mental Health
Policy Planning and Systems
Administration, Finance and Health Insurance.

Number of agencies, boards, and commissions: 32, including
Clarke Institute of Psychiatry
Addiction Research Foundation
Ontario Council of Health

Approximate number of public servants: 10,400
Approximate expenditure budget: $11.2 billion

Ministry of Skills Development

The objectives of the Ministry of Skills Development are: to develop and upgrade skills which will enhance the employability of individuals; to contribute to Ontario's economic growth by helping employers develop the skills of their staff; to improve access to training and employment opportunities for persons with special needs and for targeted groups that encounter particular employment barriers; and to coordinate institutional and on-the-job training programs in order to increase training effectiveness and employment mobility.

Divisions:
Skills Development
Youth Employment
Policy and Planning
Finance and Administration

Number of agencies, boards and commissions: 1
Institute for Skills Development

Approximate number of public servants: 480

Approximate expenditure budget: $446 million

SPECIAL PROGRAMS

In addition to the ministries and central agencies described above, five special programs: the Ontario Women's Directorate, the Ontario Native Affairs Directorate, the Office of Francophone Affairs, the Office for Senior Citizens' Affairs, and the Office for Disabled Persons operate autonomously within the Ontario government. A brief description of the roles and functions of each is given below.

Office Responsible for Women's Issues (Ontario Women's Directorate)

The Ontario Women's Directorate, under the Minister Responsible for Women's Issues, fosters the economic, social, and legal equality of women in Ontario by working with the ministries and agencies of the government to identify gaps in existing programs and to point out policies and practices which may inadvertently disadvantage women, and by developing programs which actively assist women in achieving equality.

Branches:
Consultative Services
Policy and Research
Program Development
Public Education Programs and Services

Number of agencies, boards, and commissions: 1
Ontario Advisory Council on Women's Issues

Approximate number of public servants: 50
Approximate expenditure budget: $18 million

Ontario Native Affairs Directorate

The Ontario Native Affairs Directorate coordinates government policy development with respect to Native peoples in Ontario and coordinates communications between the government and Native organizations, under the auspices of the Attorney General, who is the Minister Responsible for Native Affairs.

Approximate number of public servants: 15
Approximate expenditure budget: $4 million

Office of Francophone Affairs

The Office of Francophone Affairs advises the government on matters concerning the francophone population in the province, and coordinates French language policy within the government, under the Minister Responsible for Francophone Affairs. The Office of Francophone Affairs is situated within Cabinet Office, and its staff and expenditure budget are part of that central agency.

Office for Senior Citizens' Affairs

The Office for Senior Citizens' Affairs, under the Minister Responsible for Senior Citizens' Affairs, is responsible for developing government policy and programs for senior citizens.

Number of agencies, boards, and commissions: 1
Ontario Advisory Council on Senior Citizens.

Approximate number of public servants: 20
Approximate expenditure budget: $5 million

Office for Disabled Persons

The Office for Disabled Persons, under the Minister Responsible for Disabled Persons, attempts to increase awareness of the abilities and needs of disabled persons in society, and coordinates government efforts to respond to issues of concern to such individuals.

Number of agencies, boards, and commissions: 1
Ontario Advisory Council for Disabled Persons

Approximate number of public servants: 30

Approximate expenditure budget: $4 million

For a fuller discussion of the background, roles and functions, organization, programs, budget, agencies, boards, commissions, and legislation covered by each line ministry see George G. Bell and Andrew D. Pascoe, *The Ontario Government: Structure and Functions* (Toronto: Wall & Thompson, 1988), from which this book has been excerpted.

For more information on the composition of the Public Service, see *Annex B, Annex C* and *Annex D*. For a detailed list of the Ministers, Deputy Ministers, and Principal Officers of these Ministries and Agencies, as of March 1988, see *Annex E*.

AGENCIES, BOARDS, COMMISSIONS, AND SPECIAL PURPOSE BODIES

There are several categories of agencies, boards, commissions (ABCs), and special purpose bodies in the Government of Ontario:

Agencies, Boards, and Commissions

Agencies, Boards, Commissions, Institutes, Foundations, Tribunals, Councils, or Crown corporations are created under specific Acts, and are administered by and/or report to an appropriate Government ministry. Although Ontario lacks a formal legal definition of an agency comparable to that in the federal *Financial Administration Act,* the Committee on Government Productivity (COGP) report of 1972 laid the groundwork for a system of classifying and administering agencies, boards, and commissions in order to ensure appropriate accountability to the Government, the Legislature, and the people of Ontario. At present, there are 248 ABCs in the Ontario government. The 203 "Schedule I," agencies are those which are financially supported by the Government, and to which the Cabinet appoints some or all directors or members through an Order-in-Council. The 20 "Schedule II" agencies are self-supporting, fully operational Crown corporations, such as Ontario Hydro and the Ontario Lottery Corporation, which operate at arm's length from the the government. The 25 "Schedule III" agencies are social/cultural or research enterprises, such as the Royal Ontario Museum or the Ontario Cancer Institute, which are funded in part by the government and in part through their own public fundraising initiatives. Agencies, Boards, and Commissions perform three basic functions: Advisory (85 ABCs, including the Advisory Council on Women's Issues and the Advisory Council on Occupational Health and Safety), Regulatory (90 ABCs, including the Liquor Licence Board of Ontario and the Ontario Securities Commission), and Operational (73 ABCs, including GO Transit, and Ontario Place Corporation). Agencies vary in size and activity. They are generally created to improve administrative or operational flexibility, to deliver programs or services which cross jurisdictional boundaries of government ministries, to respond quickly to a political issue, or to secure independence from day-to-day government control.

A more detailed description of the functions of each of the major agencies, boards, and commissions in the Government of Ontario may be found in George G. Bell and Andrew D. Pascoe, *The Ontario Government: Structure and Functions* (Toronto: Wall & Thompson, 1988), from which this book has been excerpted.

Royal Commissions

Royal Commissions are investigatory bodies appointed by an Order-in-Council under the *Public Inquiries Act* to investigate a specific public concern, such as a sudden or catastrophic event (e.g. Royal Commission on Grand River Flood or Royal Commission on High Rise Fires), the conduct and activities of public service employees (e.g. Royal Commission concerning Police Activities), areas of government policy (e.g. Royal Commission on Freedom of Information and Individual Privacy or Royal Commission on Confidentiality of Health Records), or a public safety issue (e.g. Royal Commission on Health and Safety of Asbestos Workers in Ontario). The *Public Inquiries Act* is administered by the Attorney General, who governs the methods and procedures used by a Royal Commission, such as subpoena powers and hearings. Royal Commissions report to Cabinet; over 30 different Commissions have been appointed since 1973.

Judicial Inquiries

A final category of special purpose body is comprised of Judicial Inquiries, or tribunals, which are short term appointments under the *Court of Justice Act*, designed to examine complaints arising from the conduct of a provincial judge. In such circumstances, a judicial council (a panel of judges) examines the complaint or allegations, and makes a recommendation to the Attorney General concerning the appointment of a Supreme Court judge to lead a public Judicial Inquiry.

ANNEXES

ANNEXES

Annex A:
Legislative Support Services

- One office per member; the Legislative Assembly provides equipment and supplies.
- $98,883 per annum salary allowance for staff; members do their own hiring, with no restriction on the number of staff.
- Unlimited volume of mail service; unlimited local and long distance telephone service.
- $15,400 per annum allowance for constituency (riding) office rental, renovation, postage, operation and maintenance, advertising, staff travel, and miscellaneous expenses.
- $11,450 Toronto accommodation allowance for out-of-town MPPs.
- Staff in the constituency offices are hired under same staff allowance as those in the Legislative office. Partisan political activity is not permitted in the constituency offices.
- Caucus Offices: each party has a caucus office to provide services to the elected party members and to field inquiries from the public. Caucus office funding levels are established by the Board of Internal Economy, based on party standings (i.e. number of seats held in the Legislative Assembly).
- Research services:
  a. Legislative Library: 84 employees (15 researchers): non-partisan research for MPPs, committees.
  b. Each member may hire a personal research assistant.
  c. Caucus research staff:
     Government: 15
     Opposition: 10
     Third party: 10
- *Hansard* Reporting Service: provides final printed version of Assembly proceedings within 48 hours; 10 days for committee proceedings.
- Computerization of members' offices: Members Office Automation/Networking System, located in all members offices, caucus offices, all offices and departments of the Legislative Assembly, and constituency offices. Word processing, electronic mail, customized correspondence, data processing, interface with *Hansard*. Assembly business papers and bills available.

Annex B:

Remuneration for Members of the Legislative Assembly

Basic Salary for all Members: $52,400 ($33,229 sessional indemnity plus $12,616 tax free allowance)

Additional indemnities:

Premier:	$ 48,367
Minister:	28,743
Minister without Portfolio:	14,433
Parliamentary Assistant:	8,880
Opposition Leader:	33,684
Third Party Leader:	16,902
Speaker:	21,217
Deputy Speaker:	8,880
Standing Committee Chairman	4,810

Members also receive per diems and allowances for committee work, travel, and accommodation.

Source: Legislative Assembly Administration Office

Remuneration Ranges for Senior Public Servants

Deputy Ministers	$79,000 – 113,000
Assistant Deputy Ministers	$68,800 – 86,000
Executive Directors	$63,700 – 79,600
Executive Co-ordinators	$57,500 – 71,800
Branch Directors	$48,800 – 60,900

Source: Human Resources Secretariat

Annex C:
Classified Civil Servants and 1987-88 Expenditure Estimates
by Ministry and Central Agency

	Civil Servants	Expenditure Estimates
Agriculture and Food	1,711	$ 559,203,838
Attorney General	3,410	346,682,638
Cabinet Office	89	8,657,400
Citizenship	260	40,218,833
Colleges and Universities	241	2,394,402,800
Community and Social Services	8,873	3,496,461,138
Consumer and Commercial Relations	1,667	126,611,938
Correctional Services	5,856	363,842,000
Culture and Communications	401	221,294,499
Disabled Persons	27	4,432,825
Education	1,472	4,366,894,238
Energy	221	44,092,000
Environment	1,714	412,020,638
Financial Institutions	297	37,564,700
Government Services	2,903	520,498,138
Health	10,381	11,231,672,638
Housing	885	366,293,538
Industry, Trade and Technology	640	253,994,738
Intergovernmental Affairs	69	7,471,100
Labour	1,549	104,081,138
Management Board of Cabinet	341	208,654,338
Municipal Affairs	419	928,875,038
Native Affairs	13	4,379,800
Natural Resources	3,660	531,171,938
Northern Development and Mines	439	243,406,406
Revenue	3,902	736,148,606
Senior Citizens' Affairs	19	4,591,825
Skills Development	479	446,247,938
Solicitor General (including O.P.P.)	6,165	393,569,638
Tourism and Recreation	654	185,100,938
Transportation	8,466	1,832,730,038
Treasury and Economics	391	4,347,933,132
Women's Issues	53	17,942,800
Totals:	**67,667**	**$ 34,787,143,210**

Note: The staff total does not include the Provincial Auditor, Office of the Ombudsman, the Legislative Assembly, or the Office of the Premier, as they do not employ public servants.

Source: Human Resources Secretariat, March 1988.

Annex D:
Classified Service by Age and Salary

Salary in $	under 25	25–34	35–44	45–54	55–64	65+	Total	%
under 15,000	59	120	147	150	371	9	856	1.2
15,000–19,999	769	1,853	1,378	944	1,066	25	6,035	8.8
20,000–24,999	1,295	7,311	6,461	4,202	3,566	54	22,899	33.2
25,000–29,999	482	3,304	3,561	2,290	1,745	22	11,404	16.6
30,000–34,999	81	3,019	3,892	2,541	1,619	22	11,174	16.3
35,000–39,999	22	1,774	3,135	1,829	846	14	7,620	11.1
40,000–44,999	0	494	1,377	936	483	3	3,293	4.8
45,000 +	0	298	2,261	1,790	1,174	35	5,558	8.1
Total	2,708	18,173	22,212	14,682	10,870	184	68,829	100.0
percentage	3.9	26.4	32.2	21.3	15.8	0.3	100.0	

There are 39,024 males (56.7%) and 29,805 females (43.3%) in the Ontario public service. Average salary for males is $32,170, while the average salary for females is $24,921.

Source: Civil Service Commission, Annual Report, 1986.

Annex E:
Ministers, Deputy Ministers, and Principal Officers
(as of March, 1988)

Office of the Premier:

Room 281
Queen's Park
Toronto, Ontario
M7A 1A1   (416) 965-1941

Premier: *Honourable David Peterson*
Executive Director: *Gordon Ashworth*
Principal Secretary: *Hershel Ezrin*

Cabinet Office:

Room 381
Queen's Park
Toronto, Ontario
M7A 1A1   (416) 965-1945

Chairman of Cabinet: *Honourable Murray Elston*
Secretary of Cabinet and Clerk of the Executive
      Council: *Robert Carman*
Government House Leader: *Honourable Sean Conway*

ECONOMIC POLICY MINISTRIES:

1. Ministry of Agriculture and Food:

11th Floor
801 Bay Street
Toronto, Ontario
M7A 1A2   (416) 965-1041

Minister: *Honourable Jack Riddell*
Deputy Minister: *Dr. Clayton Switzer*
Parliamentary Assistant: *Gordon Miller*

2. Ministry of Energy:

12th Floor
56 Wellesley Street West
Toronto, Ontario
M7A 2B7   (416) 965-4286

Minister: *Honourable Robert Wong*
Deputy Minister: *Donald Crosbie*
Parliamentary Assistant: *none*

3. Ministry of Environment:

15th Floor
135 St. Clair Avenue West
Toronto, Ontario
M4V 1P5   (416) 323-4359

Minister: *Honourable James Bradley*
Deputy Minister: *Gary Posen*
Parliamentary Assistant: *Christine Hart*

4. Ministry of Housing:

10th Floor
777 Bay Street
Toronto, Ontario
M5G 2E5   (416) 585-7111

Minister: *Honourable Chaviva Hosek*
Deputy Minister: *Gardner Church*
Parliamentary Assistant: *Maurice Bossy*

5. Ministry of Industry, Trade and Technology:

Minister: *Honourable Monte Kwinter*
Deputy Minister: *Patrick Lavelle*
Parliamentary Assistant and Small Business
    Advocate: *Rick Ferraro*

8th Floor
900 Bay Street
Toronto, Ontario
M7A 2E1   (416) 965-1617

. **Ministry of Labour:**

Minister: *Honourable Gregory Sorbara*
Deputy Minister: *Glenn Thompson*
Parliamentary Assistant: *Shirley Collins*

14th Floor
400 University Avenue
Toronto, Ontario
M7A 1T7   (416) 965-4101

7. Ministry of Municipal Affairs:

Minister: *Honourable John Eakins*
Deputy Minister: *Donald Obonsawin*
Parliamentary Assistant: *Dave Neumann*

17th Floor
777 Bay Street
Toronto, Ontario
M5G 2E5   (416) 585-7000

8. Ministry of Natural Resources:

Minister: *Honourable Vincent Kerrio*
Deputy Minister: *George Tough*
Parliamentary Assistant: *James McGuigan*

6th Floor
99 Wellesley Street West
Toronto, Ontario
M7A 1W3   (416) 965-1301

9. Ministry of Northern Development and Mines:

Minister of Northern Development:
Honourable Rene Fontaine
Minister of Mines: *Honourable Sean Conway*
Deputy Minister: *Brock Smith*
Parliamentary Assistants:
Taras Kozyra (Northern Development)
Sterling Campbell (Mines)

10th Floor
10 Wellesley Street East
Toronto, Ontario
M4Y 1G2   (416) 965-1417

10. Ministry of Tourism and Recreation:

Minister: *Honourable Hugh O'Neil*
Deputy Minister: *James Keenan*
Parliamentary Assistant: *Harry Pelissero*

7th Floor
77 Bloor Street West
Toronto, Ontario
M7A 2R9   (416) 963-1401

11. Ministry of Transportation:

Minister: *Honourable Edward Fulton*
Deputy Minister: *David Hobbs*
Parliamentary Assistant: *Tony Lupusella*

Main Floor East
1201 Wilson Avenue
Downsview, Ontario
M3M 1J8   (416) 235-4449

JUSTICE MINISTRIES:

1. **Ministry of the Attorney General:**

   Attorney General: *Honourable Ian Scott*
   Deputy Attorney General: *Richard Chaloner*
   Parliamentary Assistant: *Steven Offer*

   18th Floor
   18 King Street East
   Toronto, Ontario
   M5C 1C5   (416) 965-1664

2. **Ministry of Consumer and Commercial Relations:**

   Minister: *Honourable William Wrye*
   Deputy Minister: *Valerie Gibbons*
   Parliamentary Assistant: *Ray Haggerty*

   9th Floor
   555 Yonge Street
   Toronto, Ontario
   M7A 2H6   (416) 963-0311

3. **Ministry of Correctional Services:**

   Minister: *Honourable David Ramsay*
   Deputy Minister: *Robert McDonald*
   Parliamentary Assistant: *none*

   2001 Eglinton Avenue East
   Scarborough, Ontario
   M1L 4P1   (416) 750-3301

4. **Ministry of Financial Institutions:**

   Minister: *Honourable Robert Nixon*
   Deputy Minister: *Bryan Davies*
   Parliamentary Assistant: *Brad Nixon*

   8th Floor
   555 Yonge Street
   Toronto, Ontario
   M7A 2H6   (416) 963-6361

5. **Ministry of the Solicitor General:**

   Solicitor General: *Honourable Joan Smith*
   Deputy Solicitor General: *John Takach*
   Parliamentary Assistant: *Ron Kanter*

   11th Floor
   25 Grosvenor Street
   Toronto, Ontario
   M7A 1Y6   (416) 965-6063

SOCIAL POLICY MINISTRIES:

1. **Ministry of Citizenship:**

   Minister: *Honourable Gerry Phillips*
   Deputy Minister: *Maureen O'Neil*
   Parliamentary Assistant: *Tony Ruprecht*

   6th Floor
   77 Bloor Street West
   Toronto, Ontario
   M7A 2R9   (416) 965-6202

2. **Ministry of Colleges and Universities:**

   Minister: *Honourable Lyn McLeod*
   Deputy Minister: *Tom Brzustowski*
   Parliamentary Assistant: *Monika Turner*

   13th Floor
   101 Bloor Street West
   Toronto, Ontario
   M5S 1P7   (416) 965-6423

3. Ministry of Community and Social Services:

Minister: *Honourable John Sweeney*
Deputy Minister: *Peter Barnes*
Parliamentary Assistant: *Gilles Morin*

6th Floor
80 Grosvenor Street
Toronto, Ontario
M7A 1E9   (416) 965-2341

4. Ministry of Culture and Communications:

Minister: *Honourable Lily Munro*
Deputy Minister: *David Silcox*
Parliamentary Assistant: *none*

6th Floor
77 Bloor Street West
Toronto, Ontario
M7A 2R9   (416) 965-8098

5. Ministry of Education:

Minister: *Honourable Christopher Ward*
Deputy Minister: *Bernard Shapiro*
Parliamentary Assistant: *Yvonne O'Neill*

22nd Floor
900 Bay Street
Toronto, Ontario
M7A 1L2   (416) 965-5277

6. Ministry of Health:

Minister: *Honourable Elinor Caplan*
Deputy Minister: *Dr. Martin Barkin*
Parliamentary Assistant: *Ken Keyes*

10th Floor
80 Grosvenor Street
Toronto, Ontario
M7A 2C4   (416) 965-2421

7. Ministry of Skills Development:

Minister: *Honourable Alvin Curling*
Deputy Minister: *Glenna Carr*
Parliamentary Assistant: *none*

13th Floor
101 Bloor Street West
Toronto, Ontario
M5S 1P7   (416) 965-8282

8. Office for Disabled Persons:

Minister Responsible for Disabled
Persons: *Honourable Remo Mancini*
Senior Adviser: *Clement Sauve*

3rd Floor
700 Bay Street
Toronto, Ontario
M5G 1Z5   (416) 965-3165

9. Office for Senior Citizens' Affairs:

Minister (without portfolio) for Senior
Citizens' Affairs: *Honourable Mavis Wilson*
Special Advisor to the Minister: *Glen Heagle*

6th Floor
76 College Street
Toronto, Ontario
M7A 1N3   (416) 965-5106

GENERAL GOVERNMENT MINISTRIES:

1. Management Board of Cabinet:

Chairman: *Honourable Murray Elston*

7th Floor
7 Queen's Park Crescent
Toronto, Ontario
M7A 1Z6 (416) 586-2020

Members: *Honourable Robert Nixon*
Treasurer and Minister of Financial Institutions
(Vice-Chairman)

Honourable James Bradley
Minister of Environment

Honourable Richard Patton
Minister of Government Services

Honourable Gerry Phillips
Minister of Citizenship

Honourable Joan Smith
Solicitor General

Honourable Robert Wong
Minister of Energy

Honourable Mavis Wilson
Minister (without Portfolio) for Senior Citizens' Affairs

Senior Officials:

Secretary of Management Board: *John Sloan*

Deputy Minister, Human Resources Secretariat: *Elaine Todres*

Chairman, Civil Service Commission: *Gerard Raymond*

2. Ministry of Government Services:

Minister: *Honourable Richard Patten*
Deputy Minister: *Dennis Caplice*
Parliamentary Assistant: *none*

12th Floor
77 Wellesley Street West
Toronto, Ontario
M7A 1N3   (416) 965-1101

3. Ministry of Intergovernmental Affairs:

Minister: *Honourable David Peterson*
Deputy Minister: *David Cameron*
Parliamentary Assistant (to the Premier
   and to the Minister of Intergovernmental
   Affairs): *Joseph Cordiano*

6th Floor
900 Bay Street
Toronto, Ontario
M7A 1C2 (416) 965-1941

4. Ministry of Revenue:

Minister: *Honourable Bernard Grandmaitre*
Deputy Minister: *Dr. Terry Russell*
Parliamentary Assistant: *none*

33 King Street West
Oshawa, Ontario
L1H 8H7   (416) 433-0870

5. Ministry of Treasury and Economics:

Minister: *Honourable Robert Nixon*
(Treasurer and Minister of Economics)
Deputy Minister: *Mary Mogford (Deputy*
Treasurer and Deputy Minister of Economics)
Parliamentary Assistant: *Claudio Polsinelli*

7th Floor
7 Queen's Park Crescent
Toronto, Ontario
M7A 1Y7   (416) 965-6361

6. Office of Francophone Affairs:

Minister Responsible for Francophone Affairs:
Honourable Bernard Grandmaitre
Minister of Revenue
Executive Director: *Remy Beauregard*

6th Floor
900 Bay Street
 Toronto, Ontario
M7A 1C2   (416) 965-3865

7. Office Responsible for Native Affairs:
(Ontario Native Affairs Directorate)

Minister Responsible for Native Affairs:
Honourable Ian Scott, Attorney General
Executive Director: *Mark Krasnick*

3rd Floor
18 King Street East
Toronto, Ontario
M5C 1C5   (416) 965-4826

8. Office Responsible for Women's Issues:
(Ontario Women's Directorate)

Minister Responsible for Women's Issues:
Honourable Gregory Sorbara, Minister of Labour
Assistant Deputy Minister: *Naomi Alboim*

2nd Floor
480 University Avenue
Toronto, Ontario
M5G 1V2   (416) 597-4500

Annex F:
Membership on Committees of Cabinet

PORTFOLIO MINISTER

	Policy & Priorities Board	Management Board	Economic Policy	Social Policy	Justice	Regulations	Legislation	Northern Development	Native Affairs	Race Relations	Emergency Planning	
Premier	C											David Peterson
Deputy Premier	*	V	C		*							Robert Nixon
Government House Leader	*		*				*	*				Sean Conway
Chairman of Cabinet	*	C								*	*	Murray Elston

ECONOMIC POLICY

	Policy & Priorities Board	Management Board	Economic Policy	Social Policy	Justice	Regulations	Legislation	Northern Development	Native Affairs	Race Relations	Emergency Planning	
Agriculture and Food			*					*				Jack Riddell
Energy		*	*							*		Robert Wong
Environment	*	*	*					*		*		James Bradley
Housing	*		*	*					*	*		Chaviva Hosek
Industry, Trade and Technology			*			V		*		*		Monte Kwinter
Labour			*		C			*	*	*		Gregory Sorbara
Mines	*		*				*	*				Sean Conway
Municipal Affairs			*				*	*		*		John Eakins
Natural Resources			*					*	*	*		Vincent Kerrio
Northern Development	*		*					C	*			Rene Fontaine
Tourism and Recreation			*					*	*			Hugh O'Neil
Transportation			*				*					Edward Fulton

JUSTICE

	Policy & Priorities Board	Management Board	Economic Policy	Social Policy	Justice	Regulations	Legislation	Northern Development	Native Affairs	Race Relations	Emergency Planning	
Attorney General	*				C		C		C	*	*	Ian Scott
Consumer & Comm. Relations					*	*				*		William Wrye
Correctional Services					*			*	*	*		David Ramsay
Financial Institutions	*	V	C		*							Robert Nixon
Solicitor General		*			*			*	*	C		Joan Smi

SOCIAL POLICY

	Policy & Priorities Board	Management Board	Economic Policy	Social Policy	Justice	Regulations	Legislation	Northern Development	Native Affairs	Race Relations	Emergency Planning	
Community and Social Services				*		V		*	*	*		John Sweeney
Citizenship		*		*	*			*	*	C		Gerry Phillips
Culture and Communications				*					*			Lily Munro
Colleges and Universities				*				*	*	*		Lynn McLeod
Education				*					*	*		Christopher Ward
Health	*			C					*		*	Elinor Caplan
Skills Development			*	*					*	*		Alvin Curling
Senior Citizen's Affairs			*	*								Mavis Wilson
Disabled Persons				*			*					Remo Mancini

GENERAL GOVERNMENT

	Policy & Priorities Board	Management Board	Economic Policy	Social Policy	Justice	Regulations	Legislation	Northern Development	Native Affairs	Race Relations	Emergency Planning	
Chairman of Management Board	*	C								*	*	Murray Elston
Government Services		*										Richard Patton
Intergovernmental Affairs	C											David Peterson
Revenue			*					*				Bernard Grandmaitre
Treasury and Economics	*	V	C		*							Robert Nixon
Francophone Affairs			*					*				Bernard Grandmaitre
Native Affairs	*				C		C		C	*	*	Ian Scott
Women's Issues			*			C		*		*	*	Gregory Sorbara

* = Committee member
C = Chairman
V = Vice Chairman

Annex G:
Premiers of Ontario 1867 – 1988

1867 – 1871	John Sandfield Macdonald (Conservative)
1871 – 1872	Edward Blake (Liberal)
1872 – 1896	Sir Oliver Mowat (Liberal)
1896 – 1899	Arthur S. Hardy (Liberal)
1899 – 1904	George W. Ross (Liberal)
1904 – 1914	James P. Whitney (Conservative)
1914 – 1919	William H. Hearst (Conservative)
1920 – 1923	Ernest C. Drury (United Farmers Of Ontario)
1923 – 1930	George H. Ferguson (Conservative)
1930 – 1934	George S. Henry (Conservative)
1934 – 1942	Mitchell F. Hepburn (Liberal)
1942 – 1943	Gordon D. Conant (Liberal)
1943 – 1944	Harry C. Nixon (Liberal)
1944 – 1948	George A. Drew (Conservative)
1948 – 1949	Thomas L. Kennedy (Conservative)
1949 – 1961	Leslie M. Frost (Conservative)
1961 – 1971	John P. Robarts (Conservative)
1971 – 1985	William Davis (Conservative)
1985	Frank Miller (Conservative)
1985 –	David Peterson (Liberal)

Annex H:
References

Fleming, Robert J., ed. *Canadian Legislatures: The 1986 Comparative Study.* Toronto: Office of the Assembly, Queen's Printer for Ontario, 1986.

MacDonald, Donald C. ed. *The Government and Politics of Ontario.* Scarborough: Nelson Canada, 1985. See especially Chapter 2, "The Structure of the Ontario Political System," by Richard A. Loreto; Chapter 4, "The Evolving Ontario Cabinet: Shaping the Structure to Suit the Times," by Hugh Segal; and Chapter 5, "Government by Other Means: Agencies, Boards and Commissions," by John Eichmanis and Graham White.

Mallory, James R. *The Structure of Canadian Government.*Toronto: Gage, 1984.

Ontario. Civil Service Commission. *Annual Report, 1986.* Toronto, 1986.

Ontario. Committee on Government Productivity. *Report Number Ten: A Summary.* Toronto, 1973.

Ontario. Management Board of Cabinet. *The Cabinet and Central Agencies: Roles and Responsibilities.* Toronto, 1987.

Ontario. Ministry of Government Services. *KWIC Index to Services.* Toronto, 1987.

Ontario. Ministry of Treasury and Economics. *Expenditure Estimates, 1987–1988.* Toronto, 1987.

Ontario. Ministry of Treasury and Economics. *Ontario Budget, 1987.* Toronto, 1987.

Schindeler, Frederick *Responsible Government in Ontario.* Toronto: University of Toronto Press, 1969.

INDEX